Sacred Roads
Adventures from the Pilgrimage Trail

NICHOLAS SHRADY

VIKING

VIKING

Published by the Penguin Group
Penguin Books Ltd, 27 Wrights Lane, London w8 5tz, England
Penguin Putnam Inc., 375 Hudson Street, New York, New York 10014, USA
Penguin Books Australia Ltd, Ringwood, Victoria, Australia
Penguin Books Canada Ltd, 10 Alcorn Avenue, Toronto, Ontario, Canada m4v 3b2
Penguin Books (NZ) Ltd, Private Bag 102902, NSMC, Auckland, New Zealand

Penguin Books Ltd, Registered Offices: Harmondsworth, Middlesex, England

First published 1999
10 9 8 7 6 5 4 3 2 1

Set in 12/15pt Monotype Dante
Typeset by Rowland Phototypesetting Ltd, Bury St Edmunds, Suffolk
Printed in Great Britain by Clays Ltd, St Ives plc

A CIP catalogue record for this book is available from the British Library

ISBN 0−670−87714−x

For Maximilian and Sebastian

Dear God, I can see it now, why can't I see it other times, that it is you I love in the beauty of the world and in all the lovely girls and dear good friends, and it is pilgrims we are, wayfarers on a journey, and not pigs, nor angels.

Walker Percy, *Love in the Ruins*

Contents

Acknowledgements

I wish to express my gratitude above all to the countless individuals who offered this pilgrim shelter, succour and sustenance along the Way; their generosity and sacrifice helped to restore my faith in humankind, not to speak of God.

In addition, my sincere thanks to: the late Agehananda Bharati, Fernando Bustos, OFM, Stephanie Cabot, Michael Carlisle, Michael Carr, Peter Carson, Mark Chimsky, Christopher and Leslie Cooke, Alfonso Echegaray, Bet Figueras, Andrew Kidd, Michael Millard, Ned O'Gorman, Eva Ortega Adell, Jack and Hania Persekian, Josep Querol Pugnaire, Per Soehlke, Michael Thomas, Michael Wollaeger, George Wright, and, of course, my mother.

Introduction

The urge to undertake a pilgrimage is both ancient and
universal. The Egyptians made their way to Sekket's shrine at
Bubastis; the Greeks sought counsel from Apollo at Delphi and
the cures of Asclepius at Epidaurus. Quetzal, Cuzco and Titicaca
were all sacred precincts in pre-Columbian America. Christian
tradition draws the faithful primarily to the Holy Land, Rome,
Santiago de Compostela, Fatima, Lourdes, and more recently, to
Medjugorje, Bosnia, where the Virgin Mary is purported to
appear daily to a group of village seers. In the Islamic world, the
pilgrim's obligatory journey or *hajj* to Mecca is one of the Five
Pillars of Faith. Buddhists venture to Bodh Gaya where the
Buddha attained enlightenment; Jews bow in prayer before the
Western Wall of the Temple; and Hindus bathe in the ash-filled
waters of the sacred Ganges. Every religion possesses its pre-
scribed rites and rituals, but pilgrimage, in particular, seems to
appeal to an instinctive movement of the human heart. The
Latin phrase *ambulare pro Deo*, 'to walk for God', is as valid for a
Christian pilgrim setting out for Santiago de Compostela as for a
Muslim drawn to the Ka'ba shrine at Mecca, or a Buddhist
circumambulating a *stupa*.

The explorer and the traveller, not to mention the tourist,
may take to a pilgrimage route, but the motives for their departure, what they seek, and the significance of their ultimate
destination are never those of a pilgrim. The pilgrim's progress is
both an interior journey, a spiritual exercise, and a physical journey towards an actual site imbued with a divine character. The
condition of the pilgrim, in fact, comes remarkably close to that
of the hero. By abandoning familiar, worldly surroundings,

submitting oneself to physical hardship and sometimes considerable danger, and paying homage or penance at a holy site, pilgrims, like heroes, know that they will return from their odyssey in some way renewed, or at least inwardly changed. 'A visitor passes through a place;' wrote Cynthia Ozick, 'the place passes through the pilgrim.' In describing mystical experience, Meister Eckhart used pilgrimage as a metaphor: 'the Wayless Way, where the Sons of God lose themselves and, at the same time, find themselves.' That, in a phrase, is every pilgrim's goal.

Ten years ago, I walked the breadth of northern Spain along the Way of St James, the ancient and arduous pilgrimage route that leads to Santiago de Compostela, where the remains of St James the Apostle are said to rest in the cathedral crypt. The 500-mile, month-long journey, I have increasingly come to realize, was a seminal event in my life. Along the pilgrimage trail, episodes and encounters unfolded with the clarity of parables. I was variously taken in by shepherds, gypsies, country priests, and nuns under vows of silence. I was shut out by one of the archbishop's underlings. I walked through unsullied landscapes of immense beauty and the dark, labyrinthine medieval quarters of Pamplona, Burgos, and Leon. I encountered living saints and misanthropes. I harvested apples and olives, joined a wedding party, and nursed a vagabond through a particularly vicious bout of delirium tremens. But more than anything else, I had the opportunity to reflect and to meditate. The Way of St James was not only a taxing physical journey, but a spiritual exercise.

Although I was born and reared a Catholic, my faith was, and remains, full of profound doubts, but the pilgrimage did help to satiate an ever-increasing, if ill-defined, sense of spiritual longing. As a Christian one is taught that God is ever-present. There is, in fact, no firm theological basis to journey to any sacred site. Ancient Christianity was a religion devoid of temples, priests, sanctuaries, ceremony, and certainly pilgrimages. God is to be worshipped neither in Jerusalem nor in Gerizim, according to the Johannine Gospel, but in spirit and truth. The fact remains, however, that never had I previously felt so near to the Absolute as when I was bound to a sacred path – not in any church, confessional, or moment of solitary prayer. As I progressed towards Santiago, I came to regard the conventional world from which I was at least temporarily removed as chaotic and aimless; the world of the pilgrimage, by contrast, was, despite often precarious conditions, marked by a purity of focus. I found the Way strewn with subtle epiphanies and that, I realized, was miraculous enough. If I felt somehow blessed, it was because the pilgrimage brought me closest to Man's first condition.

I sought out other pilgrimage routes, not only in the Christian world, but in the Buddhist, Hindu, Jewish, and Islamic traditions as well. The notion that God or the Absolute can be approached while journeying, I discovered, is all but universal. It is telling, for example, that Yahweh means the 'God of the Way'; or that in Arabic *Il-Rah*, originally used to signify a migration path, was later appropriated by the Sufi mystics to describe 'the Way to God'. Christ and his Apostles *walked* the hills and valleys of Palestine. The quest for Zen is also referred to as *angya*, or 'going on foot'. Early Buddhists were 'wandering alms-seekers'; and their master's last words to his followers were, appropriately enough, 'Walk on!' The potential pilgrim is unlikely to find two better words of advice.

1 / A Christmas with the Virgin in Bosnia

By their fruits you will know them. *Matthew 7:16*

The military truck groaned and lurched along in low gear through the ghostly fog that hung over the road and shrouded the entire Neretva river valley of Bosnia with the ashen pallor of the dead. I was sitting in the cab between two young Spanish legionnaires who had taken me on after having crossed the border from Croatia. They were peacekeepers, but they didn't much like their mission. They had, after all, been trained to fight. There was a bullet hole in the windshield directly in front of me.

'Do you know what our unofficial motto is?' asked the soldier to my right with a rifle propped up between his knees.

'Tell me,' I said.

And suddenly they both growled in perfect unison: '*Viva la muerte!*' (Long live death).

They must have felt in their element. Whenever the fog lifted along a brief stretch of the road, I caught glimpses of the charred, rusted shells of cars, bullet-pocked walls, and mounds upon mounds of rubble.

We were smoking cheap black tobacco, and swigging exorbitantly expensive Scotch from the bottle. There was little conversation, but the driver, who had exuberant muttonchop sideburns and a smooth, ghastly scar which ran from his temple straight to the edge of his mouth, did curse incessantly and imaginatively. His unrepeatable obscenities didn't seem to be directed at anything in particular, just the fog, the road, the night, or perhaps the fact that we were all far from home on Christmas Eve.

I had walked out of Dubrovnik in a driving rain three days earlier, bound for Medjugorje. The Virgin Mary, Mother of God, it was said, had been appearing and speaking to a group of young seers from the remote Bosnian village since 1981. There was talk of miracles, of cures, of conversions and repentance, and of messages of peace and prayer before an impending Apocalypse. In the last fifteen years, twenty million pilgrims had responded to the call and journeyed to Medjugorje, a phenomenon by any standards. Still, I wasn't sure if I was marching to the scene of genuine apparitions, or to a kind of contemporary spiritual circus, like a revival under the big top.

The legionnaires dropped me off beside the road which led to Medjugorje. It was nearly two o'clock on Christmas morning. As they drove off to Mostar, I found myself surrounded by utter darkness. I stumbled towards the village, unnerved by the occasional burst of automatic gunfire and the howling of dogs woken from their slumber.

When I reached the village, I passed under a banner strung across the road which read: MEDJUGORJE: OASIS OF PEACE, and in the early morning hours, it was. There wasn't a soul to be seen. But for a few strings of festive lights, the place was dark. I knocked at the front door of a hotel, but no one appeared. I moved on to a guest house where a sign announced vacant rooms in half a dozen languages, including Korean, but I only managed to inspire a tirade in Serbo-Croat from a shadowy figure in a second-floor window. The proverbial inn, it seemed, was full.

I continued along Medjugorje's main street until I made out the twin spires of St James's church. My spirits rose. What better place to seek shelter on Christmas morning than the House of the Lord? I saw myself comfortably stretched out in a pew. The doors, however, were locked, all of them. The scent of incense and snuffed candles still lingered from midnight mass. If only I had arrived several hours earlier, I would have been happily enveloped in the fold. Just as I was asking for forgiveness for a string of curses, I detected a robed figure smoking by the adjacent parish house. I approached and promptly startled a Franciscan brother out of his wits.

'Who are you?' he whispered harshly in a pronounced Serbo-Croat accent.

'A pilgrim,' I replied.

'It's nearly three o'clock in the morning. What are you doing wandering about?'

'I've just arrived from Dubrovnik. I'm looking for a room.'

'Aren't you with a group?'

'No, I'm alone.'

'How did you get here?'

It felt disagreeable to be grilled in the dark by someone whose face I couldn't see. 'I walked mostly.'

'Why?' he persisted.

'I suppose, when I walk, I feel closer to God.'

There was an uncomfortable, protracted silence during which I stood futilely awaiting a gesture of old-fashioned succour, and the good Franciscan smoked nervously. And then, stamping out his cigarette with the sole of his humble sandal, he volunteered, 'Well, there's no place for you here. You'll have to find a hotel.'

'Perhaps you could suggest one?' I asked.

'No, I cannot,' he replied with thorough indifference. 'I'm not from here.'

And in an instant, his robed silhouette turned and disappeared inside the shadows of the parish house. As I walked away dejected, I heard him firmly bolt the door, twice.

I wandered about aimlessly until I stumbled upon a life-size manger scene constructed behind the church for the local Christmas festivities. Naturally, I bolted for the 'inn', but it proved a pure sham, a mere façade. The stable, however, had a pitched roof covered with sweet-smelling pine boughs, and a floor strewn with dry hay. The crib for the Christ Child was empty. I fell into a corner, exhausted, and sunk into a deep, biblical slumber.

I was being kicked, not violently, but emphatically in my side. I thought that I was dreaming, but no. Through half-closed eyes, I squinted up at an old, cassock-clad priest looming above me. Anger had flushed his ruddy face the colour of claret; spittle was flying from his mouth. He railed at me in French for my sleeping arrangement. I had, he insisted, defiled a symbolic place, a miraculous place, a place of immeasurable sanctity. Behind him stood a pack of pilgrims gawking. I was not, needless to say, the Infant wrapped in swaddling clothes which they and their irate spiritual guide had expected to find in the manger. Someone, rather insensitively I thought, took a picture. I heard voices muttering, *Mais c'est possible . . . un misérable . . .* I couldn't conjure up enough of my schoolboy French to dispute the priest's ill-founded notion of consecrated ground, so I quietly and shamefully fled, pulling hay from my hair as I went.

It was Christmas Day. The ground was covered with frost, and the sky was leaden and sunless. Smoke was spiralling from the chimneys of the village, filling the air with an acrid scent and a yellow-tinged haze. The houses were whitewashed, with red tile roofs; most of them looked new, and more, many more were under construction. On the outskirts of the village lay barren and fallow fields, and rows of trellised grape vines. A colossal, concrete cross rose on the treeless summit of Mt Krizevac; it must have been visible for miles around. A relic of the true Cross was built into the reinforced concrete when the cross was erected in 1933. Medjugorje's piety was manifest long before the arrival of the Virgin.

I tried to wash at a spigot behind the church, but the pipes were frozen. So was I. Christmas had never been so exacting, or, I imagined, more relevant.

There was a Croatian mass underway inside St James's, and it was standing room only. For the benefit of those left outside, the mass came through piercing, static-filled loudspeakers. On the broad esplanade in front of the church, groups of pilgrims stood snapping photos, praying, singing, and dodging the firecrackers which a pack of mischievous village boys were tossing at their heels. They variously shrieked in English, French, German, Italian, Spanish, Korean and Japanese. The locals didn't flinch.

English mass wasn't due to be celebrated until noon, so I set off in search of lodging. A young Franciscan directed me to the House of Peace, a mean-looking contemporary edifice that was used by the parish for prayer retreats, but it was full. I went on to the imposing, three-star Kompas Apro, although I was quite sure that I couldn't afford the luxury. The young woman behind the reception desk was good enough to inform me that the hotel offered private baths, a restaurant, satellite TV, laundry services, and had reservations for the next six months. At a score of smaller hotels and rooming houses along the main street, all of which had the common feature of appearing as if they had been built in a hurry and not quite finished, I had no better luck. Medjugorje, I was beginning to realize, was not the sort of sacred site where one arrived on foot and unannounced, but rather in a Mercedes bus with confirmed reservations.

I must have looked slightly forlorn, because a gentleman approached me with an air of compassion mixed with pity. He had fine silver hair and arctic-blue eyes, and while he was well turned out in wool and tweed, his hands, I could see at once, had known work.

5

'You need room?' he asked.

'I do indeed!'

'Come, come, come, I have rooming house.'

It must have been the only establishment where I hadn't inquired. As we walked along, I was struck by the uniformity of commerce in Medjugorje. Apart from a travel agency, a diminutive grocery store, a handful of cafés, and the ubiquitous money changers, almost every other business seemed to be devoted to selling the whole gaudy lot of Marian paraphernalia: plastic and ceramic statues of the Virgin in every conceivable size, glittering rosary beads, hologram images (at one angle the Virgin is serene, at another she is weeping), key-rings, coffee mugs, T-shirts, books, audio and video tapes, and bumper stickers proclaiming: 'The Miracle at Medjugorje', 'Queen of Peace', 'Give Me Your Wounded Heart', and 'She Is *Your* Mother Too!' What's more, business was booming. The pious were coming out of the shops with bags brimming with the stuff.

'How was this year's harvest?' I asked my companion.

'What harvest?'

'The grape harvest,' I specified, referring to what had been, along with tobacco, the region's principal crop.

'Oh, we don't work much now in fields,' he acknowledged. 'Now, tourists big business.'

'But what if the Virgin disappears and the tourists stop coming?' I ventured.

He stopped dead in his tracks. 'Virgin goes away?' he asked desperately.

'No, no,' I assured him, 'but what if?'

'Children say Virgin in Medjugorje until the end,' he countered, referring to the six local visionaries who were now adults.

'What end?' I asked.

'End of world,' he said matter-of-factly.

The house, in fact, looked more like a building site. A small terrace which fronted the street was strewn with bags of mortar, cinder blocks, and a heap of sand. There were half a dozen plastic tables with umbrellas. 'Here, you can sit and have cool drink,' he pronounced rather optimistically. The temperature must have been near freezing.

We entered through the ground-floor bar. It seemed colder inside than on the street. The floor was of concrete, a number of windows were still without panes, and although there was a row of radiators along one wall, they seemed to be pure embellishment. The shelves behind the bar, decorated with coloured lights and tinsel, contained bottles of cheap booze, a plastic figure of the Virgin, a small Croatian flag, and an oversized portrait of Croatian strongman Franco Tudjman in a snow-white uniform with a profusion of gold braid and buttons. My host noticed me lingering before the portrait. 'We are Croats, Christians,' he offered, 'like all of Medjugorje.'

'Really?' I replied. 'Are there no Muslims in the vicinity?'

'Muslims!' he cried. 'Here, no . . . Not any more.'

'Where did they go?'

'To Bosnia.'

'We're in Bosnia,' I stated.

'They go to Muslim Bosnia!'

'Which way is that, exactly?'

But he didn't answer. He moved behind the bar and poured himself some clear liquor from a labelless bottle. He didn't invite me to join him, not that I would have accepted. He drained the glass, and then another. Neither of us said a word, but I was convinced that he wasn't going to rent me the room after all. Finally, he asked, 'What are you?'

'What do you mean?'

'Your religion.'

'I was born and raised a Roman Catholic.'

This seemed to satisfy him.

'Anna!' he bellowed without moving a step.

Presently, a young woman appeared on the threshold which led to the private quarters. She was beautiful, but looked drawn and plaintive. Her hair was black as coal and hung loose in ringlets around the fine bones of her face. When she raised her eyes, I saw that they were pale green, the colour of sage. She resembled a Byzantine Madonna. She didn't look at me. The proprietor muttered something to her in Serbo-Croat, and then said to me, 'This is the wife of my son, she take you to room.' He then poured himself another drink. His arctic-blue eyes had already lost their lustre.

My room consisted of two sagging beds and a soggy carpet. One wall was decorated with a poster of the Virgin, and another with an image of Sylvester Stallone, all muscle and sinew, and a source of inspiration, no doubt, for whoever used the weights and barbells which occupied a corner. There were gaps between the cinder blocks so gaping that there was actually a breeze, and when I exhaled, my breath appeared in great billowing plumes. Thinking that the room was a marginal improvement over the manger, if only for being spared kicks in my side, I accepted at once. Comfort, after all, is rarely a part of the pilgrim's condition.

Mass wasn't due to begin for another half-hour, but the church was already packed. I had to squeeze my way through the crowd just to occupy a tiny sliver of space along a side aisle. I looked up to find myself beneath the Sixth Station of the Cross; Veronica was wiping Christ's face with her veil.

The church, although begun in 1934, had only recently been renovated with funds provided by the pilgrims. Clearly, the planners had miscalculated, for the space was far too small for the burgeoning throng. Everything, including the pews, the confessionals and the altar, had the distinct appearance of being prefabricated. Along the left side wall, stained-glass windows depicted scenes from the life of Mary; on the right, they portrayed events associated with the apparitions.

At the head of the right aisle, just off the apse, pilgrims were pressing for a closer look at the statue of the Virgin of Medjugorje. The rendering is faithful to the visions of the Virgin described by the seers: she is cloaked in a flowing pearly-grey gown; her veil is immaculately white; her hands are clasped together in prayer; and a crown of twelve stars (first described by St John in the Book of Revelation) enshrines her flawless head and face. I thought that the statue was a conspicuous example of the decline in ecclesiastical art, but aesthetics, I reminded myself, were not the issue.

The pilgrims themselves were a curious lot. More than a few had an ecstatic, wild-eyed look; some were lying prostrate in prayer, while others were gazing heavenward with beatific smiles and arms extended in a gesture of stigmatic sacrifice. A good many of the women wore black veils and clutched rosaries in gloved hands, an image which reminded me of the masses of my youth. The most worthy of compassion, however, were the legions of sick, lame, blind, and just plain desperate souls who had journeyed to Medjugorje in the hopes of a miraculous cure or intervention from Our Lady. I had seen and spoken with others like them in Lourdes and Fatima, and their faith and hope seemed boundless. They accepted that a remote God had brought them into the world afflicted, but they were convinced that it was His mother, Virgin most merciful and comforter of the stricken, who had the power to intercede on their behalf. I thanked God that I was physically healthy and, at the same time, acknowledged that in spirit, perhaps I wasn't quite so robust as many of those gathered around me.

When mass began, there were a full dozen priests presiding at the altar. Father Ivan Landeka, the parish priest, was joined by clerics from France, Puerto Rico, Australia, Japan, Germany, Nigeria, the United States, and Croatia. Few, it seemed, had been overlooked. To accommodate the diversity of pilgrims, all of the prayers and hymns were offered in Serbo-Croat, English, French, and Italian. The texts were projected in all four languages on a wide screen in the apse so that everyone could follow. This, of course, was most considerate, but made for a slightly tedious and drawn-out mass. Still, I found the unbridled enthusiasm of the congregation most refreshing. When, for example, the liturgy called for a responsorial psalm, the assembled didn't simply comply as is so often the case in your average phlegmatic service. No, they verily shouted out their due with voices filled with zeal. It felt like hallelujah time!

I also admired the sense of fraternity displayed by the pilgrims. Throughout the entire mass, the confessionals remained open, and they were visited by a steady stream of penitents. I noticed one Croatian military officer emerge from his confession sobbing uncontrollably, and watched as a group of anonymous pilgrims promptly and spontaneously embraced and comforted him. And when it became time for the 'sign of peace', I was vigorously hugged and kissed by an elderly Italian gentleman on my right, and a burly local on my left. A beautiful French lady standing in front of me turned around and extended her elegant hand politely, and in her eyes I saw a rare sight: pure and unadulterated love.

The Christmas sermon was traditional enough. Father Landeka evoked the murderous Herod, the flight of Joseph and the Blessed Virgin, the rejection at the inn, the humble manger, and the glorious birth of the Saviour. As might have been expected, he continually emphasized Mary's blessedness, her purity, her perpetual virginity, her perfect embodiment of the will of God, and her profound role as the eternal Mother of God and the Church. The audience swooned.

Later, when the collection basket was circulated, I saw that it was stuffed with a profusion of bank notes from scores of countries, but, above all, there was an abundance of dollars, and not just single bills, but tens, twenties, fifties, and a few hundreds too. Where, I wondered, was all this hard cash going?

After we sang the four versions of the rousing 'Joy to the World' (the French rendition came off best owing to the presence of a full choir from Normandy), Father Ivan announced rather casually, along with a reminder of catechism classes and details of a fund-raising drive for war refugees, that the monthly message from the Virgin would be offered under the tent behind the church later that evening. After fifteen years of apparitions, the miraculous had become somewhat routine.

It all started with the prophet Elijah. In the spring of 1981, one month before the apparitions of the Virgin began in Medjugorje, villagers reported that they had witnessed Elijah riding his flaming chariot drawn by flaming horses across the balmy evening sky of Bosnia. It was an unequivocal sign, an omen, a prophetic vision, but of what exactly they weren't quite sure.

The prophet Elijah (a Hebrew name meaning 'Yah[weh] is God') is one of the Old Testament's most sanguinary characters, a messenger of wrath, a summoner of fire from heaven, and, curiously enough, a denouncer of false gods and superstitions. But tradition also has it that Elijah, while at prayer on the heights of Mount Carmel in Palestine, was the first to witness an apparition of the Blessed Mother and her Divine Son, nearly a millennium before they walked the earth. He is a vital link between the Old Testament and the New, and the one prophet who has always been awaited and evoked with anticipation, for he never passed through the gates of death, but 'went up on a whirlwind into heaven' (IV Kings 2:11). He is expected to return, as Christ

told Peter, James and John on Mount Tabor, 'to restore
all things as they were' (Matthew 17:11).

On 24 June 1981, the Feast of John the Baptist, one month after
Elijah had been seen in the sky over Medjugorje, a radiant light
appeared atop Mount Podbrdo overlooking the village. Dusk
was falling, and fifteen-year-old Ivanka Ivanković and sixteen-
year-old Mirjana Dragičević were strolling together after having
finished their daily chores. As the girls trained their eyes on the
light, they saw a woman bathed in shimmering rays. She was
holding an infant. Not surprisingly, their initial reaction was one
of fear, and they turned and fled. Shortly after, however, they
returned, this time accompanied by a number of friends from
the village. Again, the vision appeared. The children were awe-
struck; some prayed, knowing implicitly that they were seeing
Gospa or Our Lady; others were filled with terror and could do
nothing but cry. Soon the image disappeared, and the children
descended the mountain and ran home to tell their families what
they had seen.

In a village of scarcely four hundred families, it didn't take
long for word of the apparition to spread. The following
evening, Mirjana and Ivanka were joined by a nine-year-old boy
named Jakov Colo, and three other teenagers: Vicka Ivanković,
Marija Pavlović and Ivan Dragičević. These six would become
the nucleus of visionaries. As the children ascended Podbrdo,
they were watched from a distance by a small crowd of curious
villagers who suddenly saw the group begin to run up the mountain as if borne on wings. The children then fell to their knees,
and when the villagers approached, they saw that the six were in
a state of ecstasy. The apparition lasted close to fifteen minutes,
during which time the luminous figure in pearly grey and with
a crown of twelve stars identified herself as 'the Blessed Virgin
Mary' and beckoned the visionaries to come closer to behold the

Infant which she bore in her arms. Her parting words were, 'Go in the peace of God.'

As the children descended the mountain, now followed by an excited crowd, Marija struck out running on her own down another path. When the others reached her, they again found her in ecstasy. Marija later described how she had found herself before a radiant cross in front of which the Virgin Mary was weeping as she implored, 'Peace. Only peace! You must seek peace. There must be peace on earth! You must be reconciled with God and with each other! Peace! Only peace!'

In the days which followed, the apparitions continued, and the crowds quickly grew to a multitude. The road to Medjugorje became choked with traffic, shops closed, businesses waned, and the fields were left idle. Although Yugoslavia was still then a socialist republic, and officially secular, the country had long been tolerant of religious activities. Still, nothing had quite prepared government officials for such a popular outpouring of faith. They suspected a nationalist plot. The visionaries and their families were interrogated and subjected to psychiatric examinations (the seers were deemed utterly 'normal'); the parish priest Father Jozo Zovko was imprisoned on charges of sedition; the Franciscan Order was threatened with expulsion from the country; and St James's was sacked. The apparitions, however, continued unabated, and the villagers, now joined by legions from beyond the valley, defied police orders to stay away from the church and Podbrdo, which had now become known as Apparition Hill. Perhaps fearing that they were creating martyrs, government officials and the police loosened their grip. The respite was enough to convince the faithful that the Virgin Mary had won the battle over the dark atheist forces. The message rang out with all the force of a clarion blast. Before long, pilgrims from abroad were flocking to Medjugorje in fleets of buses, bringing hope, prayers, and something which even the socialist régime could appreciate – copious amounts of hard currency.

Short of the Second Coming of Christ, apparitions of His mother are, one might say, the next best thing. Two thousand years have passed since Jesus walked among us, too long a time for many of the faithful who thirst for a more immediate manifestation of the divine. While Christ was the Ultimate Mediator, the God made Man who interceded for humankind in the face of a remote and awe-inspiring God the Father, it is the Virgin who has increasingly come to mediate between humankind and the Saviour.

Scripture teaches that Mary followed her Son throughout His earthly presence with unfailing motherliness, but with the exception of the Magnificat assigned to her in the Gospel According to Luke – *Magnificat anima mea Dominum* ('My soul doth magnify the Lord') – her role was never highly prophetic. Yet popular identification with Mary, the Mother, has always struck a familiar chord with the faithful precisely because she has never been deemed divine. And while she is no God, and indeed has no power of her own, she is none the less fervently worshipped and glorified. In the Litany of the Blessed Virgin, Mary is attributed with a loaded string of epithets, including: Holy Virgin of Virgins, Mother of Divine Grace, Mother most chaste, Mother undefiled, Virgin most prudent, Virgin most powerful, Virgin most merciful, Mirror of Justice, Seat of Wisdom, Queen of Prophets, Queen of Angels, Queen of Martyrs, Queen conceived without original sin, Queen assumed into Heaven, and, my favourite, the simple and eloquent Queen of Peace, as she has come to be known in Medjugorje.

Although the essence of Christianity is succinctly proclaimed in the three words 'Christ has risen', to the popular imagination, the power of that transcendent message very often pales in comparison to the claim that His mother is appearing and speaking to us, albeit through visionaries and in His name, from a specific place that is a mere plane journey away. That twenty million pilgrims have made their way to Medjugorje over the last fifteen years speaks volumes of the human heart's need for something tangible with which to satiate its spiritual longing.

Since the Passion of Christ, history is rich in purported apparitions of Our Lady, and with each vision, the Marian cult, or what debunkers have often referred to sardonically as Mariolatry, has grown ever stronger. She has turned up most often, and some would say all too conveniently, when the faith has been threatened by a rival dogma, growing secularism, or a need for fresh converts. She is said to have appeared to, among others, Saint John the Apostle; a Roman soldier (later to become Emperor Leo I) while on the road to Constantinople; Saint Simon Stock, to whom she gave the brown scapular, the wearing of which is supposed to confer extraordinary graces; the soldier-turned-saint Ignatius of Loyola; the exquisite mystic poet Saint Teresa of Avila; the convert Aztec Indian Juan Diego on Tepayac Hill; the Jew Alphonse Ratisbonne, the son of a wealthy banking family, while on a visit to Rome to admire the antiquities; Bernadette Soubirous in a dank grotto in Lourdes, France; and four shepherd girls on a hillside in Fatima, Portugal. She has appeared to Christians, Jews, Muslims, Hindus, Buddhists, and Animists. At present, apparitions are being reported in Damascus, Syria; Naju, South Korea; Betania, Venezuela; and, of course, in Medjugorje. Not surprisingly, literally thousands of additional claims of apparitions and locutions have arisen from pilgrims throughout the world fresh back from pilgrimage sites, particularly Medjugorje. The Vatican, whose task it is to evaluate the authenticity of apparitions, can scarcely keep up with the flood of claims.

The Church has yet to make a definitive statement approving

or rejecting the apparitions at Medjugorje. In these, as in most matters, the Vatican moves slowly and with utmost caution. Medjugorje is not, strictly speaking, a Catholic pilgrimage place – not like Jerusalem, Rome, Santiago de Compostela, Lourdes, or Fatima, to name a few. It is, while the ecclesiastical invest-igations continue, nothing more than a destination for religious tourism. But the Church has not exactly discouraged the flock from venturing to Bosnia either. Pope John Paul II's devotion to the Virgin is well known, and he has said that he survived the attempt on his life on 13 May 1981 thanks to the Virgin of Fatima (the date coincided with the Virgin's first apparition at Fatima in 1917). He has also purportedly said that if he were not the pope, he would be hearing confessions in Medjugorje.

The Declaration of the Yugoslav Bishops' Conference on Medjugorje, held in Zadar, Croatia in 1991 stated:

> On the basis of the investigations so far, it cannot be affirmed that one is dealing with supernatural apparitions and revelations.
>
> However, the numerous gatherings of great numbers of the faithful from different parts of the world, who are coming to Med-jugorje prompted by motives of belief and various other motives, do require attention and pastoral care – in the first place by the Bishop of the diocese and with him also of the other Bishops, so that both in Medjugorje and in everything connected with it a healthy devotion to the Blessed Virgin Mary may be promoted in accord-ance with the teachings of the Church.

The crux of the declaration is clear. While the apparitions can-not be confirmed, neither are the pilgrims to be discouraged in their devotion to the Virgin, so long as their faith does not veer from established orthodoxy.

To the droves of pilgrims, however, official Vatican approval seems to be of only relative importance. What has captivated the throng and fired their faith is the persistence of the apparitions and the sheer quantity of messages which Our Lady is said to be delivering to humankind. To Saint Ignatius of Loyola, the Virgin Mary appeared but once; and to the young girls at Fatima a mere seven times. To the visionaries of Medjugorje, however, Our Lady has appeared daily since 1981. Jakov, Vicka, Marija and Ivan see her every day, and Mirjana and Ivanka once a year. Over the last fifteen years, the Virgin Mary has entrusted the seers with reams of messages which make the sum total of her previous utterances appear brief and cursory. As the Mother of God proclaimed to the six visionaries on 4 April 1985, 'I wish to continue giving you messages as never before in history since the beginning of time.'

From the start, the Mother of God elaborated a principal message which has become the touchstone of the Medjugorje experience, and can be summed up in five essential words: Peace, Faith, Prayer, Conversion, and Fasting. These dictates can be interpreted as follows:

Peace is the emulation of the Divine Life. The Virgin of Medjugorje is the Queen of Peace, and among the most common titles for her Son is the Prince of Peace.

Faith is the return of the mind to God's word and the rejection of sin, 'And Christ's mind is ours' (1 Corinthians 2:16).

Prayer is the medium through which the spirit/soul of man is united with God, 'whereas the man who unites himself to the Lord becomes one spirit with him' (1 Corinthians 6:17).

Conversion is the choice through free will to embrace the Word made Flesh, her Son, Jesus Christ.

Fasting is the call to heal the mortal body of all its sinful passions and appetites. Jesus is the Bread of Life, and water, the Holy Spirit through which the body is sanctified for everlasting life.

Subsequent messages reinforced these five pillars of the Virgin's mission, and have been delivered with uncanny reliability every Thursday from 1 March 1984 to 8 January 1987, and on the 25th of each month from 25 January 1987 to the present. The Virgin's choice of Thursdays to deliver her messages remains something of a mystery, but devotees of Medjugorje have interpreted the choice of the 25th of each month as a date highly charged with symbolism. 25 June is often the date of the summer solstice, the day of maximum light. All succeeding days diminish in light until 25 December, the Nativity of the 'Light of the world' (John 8:12). From 25 December (or winter solstice) onwards, the days begin to increase in light. Nothing at Medjugorje is random, according to the faithful, everything is part of a cosmic drama.

Herein, a selection of some of the Virgin's messages conveyed through the visionaries and 'directed to all of mankind'.

The Chosen Parish, 1 March 1984
Dear children! I have chosen this parish in a special way and I wish to lead it. I am guarding it in love and I want everyone to be mine. Thank you for having responded tonight. I wish you always to be with me and my Son in ever greater numbers. I shall speak a message to you every Thursday.

Consecration to Mary Wins Special Graces, 17 May 1984
Dear children! Today I am very happy because there are many who want to consecrate themselves to me. Thank you. You have not made a mistake. My Son, Jesus Christ, wishes to bestow on you special graces through me. My Son is happy because of your dedication. Thank you for having responded to my call.

Everyone, Priests Included, Pray the Rosary, 25 June 1985
(The following was a special message which the Virgin gave in response to Marija's question, 'Our Lady, what do you wish to recommend to the priests?')

I invite you to call on everyone to pray the rosary. With the rosary you shall overcome all the adversities which Satan is trying to inflict on the Catholic Church. All you priests, pray the rosary! Dedicate your time to the rosary!

Foiling Satan's Plan for the Fruit of the Vine, 29 August 1985
Dear children! I am calling you to prayer! Especially since Satan wishes to take advantage of the yield of your vineyards. Pray that Satan does not succeed in his plan. Thank you for having responded to my call.

Mary the Mediatrix between the Faithful and God, 17 July 1986
Dear children! Today I am calling you to reflect upon why I am with you this long. I am the Mediatrix between you and God. There- fore, dear children, I desire to call you to live always out of love all that which God desires of you. For that reason, dear children, in your own humility live all the messages which I am giving you. Thank you for having responded to my call.

Complete Surrender to God as King, 25 July 1988
Dear children! Today I am calling you to a complete surrender to God. Everything you do and everything you possess give over to God so that He can take control in your life as King of all that you possess. That way through me God can lead you into the depths of the spiritual life. Little children, do not be afraid, because I am with you even when you think there is no way out and that Satan is in control. I am bringing peace to you. I am your Mother and the Queen of Peace. I am blessing you with the blessing of joy so that for you God may be everything in life. Thank you for having responded to my call.

Dear Children! Pray! Pray! Pray!, 25 October 1991

Fasting and Prayer Can Stop the War, 25 April 1992

Dear children! Today also I invite you to prayer. Only by prayer and fasting can war be stopped. Therefore, my dear little children, pray and by your life give witness that you are mine and that you belong to me, because Satan wishes in these turbulent days to seduce as many souls as possible. Therefore, I invite you to decide for God and He will protect you and show you what you should do and which path to take. I invite all those who have said 'yes' to me to renew their consecration to my Son Jesus and to His Heart and to me so we can take you more intensely as instruments of peace in this unpeaceful world. Medjugorje is a sign to all of you and a call to pray and live the days of grace that God is giving you. Therefore, dear children, accept the call to prayer with seriousness. I am with you and your suffering is also mine. Thank you for having responded to my call.

Why This War Has Lasted So Long, 25 October 1993

Dear children! These years I have been calling you to pray, to live what I am telling you, but you are living my messages a little. You talk, but you do not live, that is why, little children, this war is lasting so long. I invite you to open yourselves to God and in your hearts to live with God, living the good and giving witness to my messages. I love you and wish to protect you from every evil, but you do not desire it. Dear children, I cannot help you if you do not live God's commandments, if you do not live the mass, if you do not give up sin. I invite you to be apostles of love and goodness. In this world of unrest give witness to God and God's love, and God will bless you and give you what you seek from Him. Thank you for having responded to my call.

Praying for Croatia and Pope John Paul II's Health, 25 August 1994

Dear children! Today I am united with you in prayer in a special way, praying for the gift of the presence of my most beloved son in your home country. Pray, little children, for the health of my most beloved son, who suffers, and whom I have chosen for these times. I pray and intercede before my Son, Jesus, so that the dream that your fathers had may be fulfilled. Pray, little children, in a special way, because Satan is strong and wants to destroy hope in your heart. I bless you. Thank you for having responded to my call.

Be Missionaries of My Messages, 25 February 1995
Dear children! Today I invite you to become missionaries of my messages, which I am giving here through this place that is dear to me. God has allowed me to stay this long with you and therefore, little children, I invite you to live with love the messages I give and to transmit them to the whole world, so that a river of love flows to people who are full of hatred and without peace. I invite you, little children, to become peace where there is no peace and light where there is darkness, so that each heart accepts the light and the way of salvation. Thank you for having responded to my call.

I sat in one of the back pews of St James's reading the messages from the Mother of God in the half-light. An ancient local woman entered carrying a single white carnation. She knelt before the statue of the Virgin, recited the rosary, and left the flower as a votive offering. As she hobbled out, I saw that tears were flowing from her milky-blue, cataract-filled eyes. A sacristan came to change the candles. Otherwise, I was alone.

There was a great deal about the messages that left me uneasy. They didn't contain anything heretical, anything to shock the orthodoxy, but to me they simply didn't ring true. I couldn't imagine that these words were divinely inspired. They were decidedly pious and full of a genuine fear of the Lord, but where was the wisdom, the knowledge, and the counsel that are said to be the authentic signs of Marian locutions? Where was the inspiration that fired Saint Teresa of Avila to write 'The Way of Perfection'? Believers would, no doubt, counter that the Virgin speaks to each visionary in the language and manner that are appropriate to them, for she is their mother too. Yet after fifteen years of daily apparitions, Our Lady was still addressing the seers as her 'little children' and exhorting them in a way which struck me as often cruel. How, for example, could the Mother of God have laid the blame for the prolongation of the war in Bosnia on the visionaries (and by extension on all of her children) because they had not prayed hard enough, or fasted long enough, or converted soon enough? The mere idea struck me as preposterous. Why indeed had she not appeared instead in downtown Belgrade?

I also detected what I thought were a number of dubious claims. In the message of 25 August 1994, the Virgin appealed for prayers for the Pope's health. All very well and good. But John Paul II then becomes the pontiff 'whom I have chosen for these times'. To my knowledge, the Virgin has never had any role in determining the successor of St Peter; that is in God's hands. In the same message, she offers a special prayer for the 'home country' Croatia (not Bosnia) and offers to intercede before her Son 'so that the dream that your fathers had may be fulfilled'. Meaning, I assumed, that Medjugorje would be incorporated into Catholic Croatia and become free at last from the predominantly Muslim Bosnia. This was hardly the sort of intercession that I expected from the 'Queen of Peace'.

I knelt to pray, not before the Virgin, but before the Cross. I prayed long and hard for insight and humility, love and compassion, but, above all, I offered a solemn, heartfelt prayer that the whole spectacle at Medjugorje was not a simple, human-inspired hoax.

I walked out of St James's in the dark and joined the crowd that was making its way to an enormous tent pitched hard by the church. Marija, the visionary, was going to appear and share with the eager throng the Virgin's latest message, a special Christmas message. The tent was full. We must have been nearly a thousand souls. The largest contingent seemed to be of Koreans (the world's fastest-growing Catholic Church), most of whom were wearing white face-masks of the kind worn in Asian capitals to keep from breathing the smog. There was no pollution, but it was bitterly cold. They were highly animated and sang muted hymns through their masks and clapped eagerly in unison. There were lots of Italians, impeccably dressed even while on pilgrimage, and a large following of rather dour-looking Poles, who were not. There didn't appear to be many locals. They must have been at home celebrating Christmas among family. I wished I was.

Suddenly, cheers rose up from the back of the crowd, and the multitude parted, making way for Marija and her entourage. She was accompanied by a hefty Franciscan and a small group of what I gathered to be American pilgrims. Marija took the stage. She was tall and gaunt with shoulder-length brown hair and dark, alert eyes. She was smartly turned out in a loden coat. A young man who seemed to be acting as MC asked for translators, and a Korean woman, an Irishman, a Pole and an Italian joined Marija on stage. They all looked highly pleased with their unexpected role. First, we were asked to join together in an English rendition of the Hail Mary. There followed a moment of silence, and then Marija took the microphone. This was what the Mother of God had purportedly told her only hours before:

Dear children! Today I am with you in a special way, holding little Jesus on my lap and invite you, little children, to open yourselves to His call. He calls you to joy. Little children, joyfully live the messages of the Gospel, which I am repeating in the time since I am with you. Little children, I am your Mother and I desire to reveal to you

the God of love and the God of peace. I do not desire for your life to
be in sadness but that it be realized in joy for eternity, according to
the Gospel. Only in this way will your life have meaning. Thank
you for having responded to my call.

The crowd cheered wildly, and again with each truncated
translation. There were shouts of 'We love you Marija!' and
'God bless the Mother of our Redeemer!' Groups of pilgrims
broke out in song, and those who couldn't follow clapped along
and swayed. As Marija descended from the stage and waded
through the crowd, pilgrims strained to take her hand and
clutched her loden coat. And then she was gone.

'Wasn't that wonderful!' proclaimed an Australian nun who
was at my side.

'What?' I asked.

'Well . . . everything,' she replied, looking at me
incredulously.

'I'm not so sure.'

She fixed me with a poisonous stare as if she were confronted with Satan himself, and then she backed away ever so
cautiously.

'Merry Christmas!' I called out to her, but she was already
swallowed up in the sea of pilgrims.

On the morning of the 26th, the Feast of Saint Stephen, I set off
for Mount Podbrdo or Apparition Hill. A cold front had swept in
from Siberia, and the wind was blowing a gale. Menacing, steel-
grey clouds rolled in a frenzy across a low sky. The path wound
through dormant vineyards. There were crows perched on the
trellises and litter caught among the naked vines. I picked up a
prayer card with an image of the Virgin on one side, and a
weathered photograph of a young boy on the other. Beneath
his tragic, hollow-eyed face were the dates of his birth and his

premature death. He hadn't made it to his sixth birthday. With a shiver, I let the card fall.

Before ascending Podbrdo, I made for the house of the visionary Vicka Ivanković, located in the hamlet of Bijakovici at the foot of the mountain. The house was painted robin's-egg blue, and had a grape arbour and climbing roses at the entrance. Smoke rose from the chimney, but the place was dark. No one answered the door. On the veranda, there were several canvas bags bulging with mail collecting mildew. There were post-marks from Asunción, Paraguay and Montreal, Jacksonville, Florida and Cologne. As I walked away, I thought I was being spied by someone from behind a lace curtain, but I didn't persist. All supposed graces aside, the burden of the visionaries must have been considerable – the letters seeking intervention from the Virgin, the droves of anonymous pilgrims turning up unan-nounced as I had, the weight of the messages, and the perpetual vigilance of the Mother of God must have required remarkable fortitude. To be chosen, I imagined, must sometimes seem a curse.

Podbrdo was as desolate as any biblical wasteland. The trail was full of scree and flanked by thorn bushes. Helpless saplings were being thrashed by the wind. There was no sound except that of the gale, but it was piercing. As I climbed, I saw that the whole slope was planted with makeshift crosses, like a forest of Calvaries. They were fashioned from planks of pine, rough-hewn branches, metal poles, and broomsticks; some were decorated with ribbons and paper flowers, or tacked with photographs of deceased loved ones. I recalled the Buddhist prayer flags on remote slopes of the Himalayas, only this scene was haunting. The only solace from the gloom came from the fine bronze bas-reliefs of the Mysteries which lined the trail and served as sources for meditation during the recitation of the rosary. I prayed at each depiction as best I could, but the truth was, I was numb with cold. Near the summit, an American woman and her three young children were kneeling before the rendering of the Fourth Glorious Mystery, the Assumption. The mother was thoroughly engrossed in prayer, but her children appeared to be on the verge of tears, their faces wincing with pain from the cold. The eldest couldn't have been more than nine years old. It was a clear act of abuse. I wanted to tell the mother that perhaps the children were a bit young to be paying penance, but when the children looked up to see me staring in disbelief, they bowed their heads in shame. Any interference on my part would likely only have made things worse. I gave the youngest girl my woollen cap, and descended Podbrdo praying through chattering teeth.

For all the evocations of peace, prayer, and reconciliation, the message from Medjugorje also includes the omen of an impending Apocalypse. Although the Mother of God has been appearing consistently for two thousand years, she has told the visionaries that her apparitions at Medjugorje are to be the last. The time, evidently, is close at hand.

Our Lady has entrusted ten secrets to the visionaries, or so they say. These secrets portend events of a terrifying, cataclysmic nature that will sweep the planet and usher in the end. All the visionaries have affirmed, incidently, that the last days will occur within their lifetime. For the unrepentant, however, it is not too late. The only secret which has been vaguely revealed is the third, which the Mother of God has told the visionaries will be a permanent, irrefutable sign at the site of the first apparition on Mount Podbrdo. Those who repent and convert in time will be saved; those who do not can expect nothing short of eternal damnation in the clutches of Satan.

Naturally, there has been feverish speculation as to the nature of the permanent sign; some have ventured that it will be a radiant church, while others insist on a column of light not unlike that with which the Jews were led out of bondage in Egypt.

For pure dramatic and poetic effect, I prefer the second option, although I should also mention that I don't believe a word of any of it. To me, conversion is a thing of the heart, not an act to which one is pushed with quaking feet and the threat of perpetual hell-fire. Warnings of an approaching Apocalypse are as old as time; fortunately, so too are unfulfilled prophecies.

At mass at St James's I listened to a fiery sermon on St Stephen, the proto-martyr falsely accused of blasphemy against the Temple and the Law, and stoned to death in the street in Jerusalem. 'Yesterday we celebrated the nativity, the coming of the "Light of the World", but today we are confronted with the blood of Stephen, and it is red and real!' ranted the priest. But it was an edifying rant. I liked his language. The predicament and courage of the early Christians seemed more real to me than anything that was going on in Medjugorje. Not once did he mention the Virgin.

After mass, I knocked at the open sacristy door as the priest was taking off his vestments and struggling to get his alb over his head.

'Come in, come in,' he said from beneath a confusion of white linen.

I helped him to free himself from his vestments.

'You must have been an altar boy.'

'For six years,' I said.

'And where was that?'

'Notre Dame church, Easton, Connecticut.'

'Here as a pilgrim, are you?'

'Of sorts.'

'What sort?' he came back quickly.

'I suppose the sceptical sort.'

He looked at me long and hard, and then the trace of a sardonic smile crossed his lips.

I liked him at once. 'I was wondering if you might have a moment to talk?' I asked.

'Naturally, but not here,' he answered, looking around as if the sacristy had ears. There was no one about, but the church was still full of pilgrims. 'We can talk in my office in the rectory.'

His name was Father Philip Pavich, OFM. His parents were Croatian, but they had emigrated to the United States before World War II, and he had grown up in Iowa. He was hefty, with a white stubble of a beard and dark penetrating eyes which he screwed up when making a cogent point or preaching from the pulpit.

For years he had served at a diminutive church in Tiberius on the shore of the Sea of Galilee, happy in the Holy Land. But duty called in Medjugorje where a priest who spoke both English and Croatian was needed to minister to the pilgrims. He didn't go reluctantly, but with glee, having long revered the Virgin.

His first few years in Medjugorje were hard, but so too was he, and he took to his new mission with a vengeance. He guided the pilgrims, dodged the communist authorities, said mass, heard confessions, and translated the Virgin's messages faithfully into English. He weathered the war. And then apostasy set in.

'I don't know with whom the visionaries are in contact, but it's not the Mother of God. I adore the Mother of God,' insisted Father Pavich as we sat in his windowless office piled high with books and manuscripts. 'The visionaries have continually implored me to preach the messages, but I cannot. I can only preach the Gospel, the word of Jesus Christ, that is my calling. Where is their legitimacy, their credibility?' he asked. 'They told me: "Spread our messages and you will be saved!" Rubbish, only God has the power to save me. My salvation is not in their hands!'

28

What truly sparked Father Pavich's disillusionment, however, were the ten secrets, and more precisely, the third. He went on to explain a tale of blunder:

The Council of Croatian Bishops, entrusted with investigating the apparitions, asked the visionaries to reveal the third secret, in which the Virgin had promised the seers a permanent sign that would confirm that the apparitions were indeed authentic. The Bishops instructed the visionaries to write down the nature of the sign on a piece of paper which would then be sealed in an envelope and kept secret. The seers refused, claiming that the Virgin forbade them from doing so. Ivan Dragičević, however, agreed, and did as he was asked. When the remaining visionaries learned that Ivan had complied, they were horrified. If the sign did not materialize, they would be discredited. Ivan panicked and promptly reneged. Not to worry, he told the others, he had given the Bishops an envelope with a blank piece of paper. Now, when the Bishops got wind of the subterfuge, it was they who were horrified. They proceeded to open the envelope and reveal what Ivan had written, namely, that a church devoted to the Virgin of Medjugorje would miraculously appear on Apparition Hill.

Needless to say, no church has appeared, miraculously or otherwise.

'But the pilgrims continue to flock here,' I said.

'You can't blame the pilgrims, or rather the religious tourists,' Father Pavich said. 'Most of them are well-meaning, although there are a good many crackpots and hangers-on for whom Medjugorje is now the centre of the universe. But the people who visit never see the truth of this place. Oasis of Peace!' he cried. 'I don't see it. What we have here is a cauldron with much hatred and primitivism.'

He buried his face in his hands and let out a weary, desperate sigh. For a long time he said nothing, but he began to shake his head.

'And the war!' he suddenly continued. 'The war brought all the horrors to the surface: heads crushed beneath the boots of Croatian soldiers; women cut open, pregnant women; whole families tortured. This is peace! And those locals shooting after Christmas mass,' he said, referring to the frenzied, commemorative shooting into the air which seemed in a sinister way to delight the villagers. 'I am horrified. It is blasphemy, an insult to Our Lord!'

'And what', I asked, 'of the visionaries?'

'Ah yes, the visionaries. They are coddled by the visiting faithful who believe them to be blessed. The locals are highly protective of them, as well they should be, since the entire local economy now relies on the pilgrims they draw. The whole business has become self-perpetuating! Each of the visionaries now has several homes; they travel; they lack nothing; and yet, none of them has a profession except that of a professional seer. What's more, they have a lifetime mandate!'

I asked him about the position of the Church.

'The Vatican will *never* approve of these apparitions,' he said emphatically. 'At least, not in the visionaries' lifetimes. Recognition would be insane! It would mean that anything these seers utter from now until their death would be regarded as revelation.'

As I stood up to leave, Father Pavich grasped my arm firmly. 'I must tell you one more thing,' he said. 'Medjugorje has touched millions of people in a profound way; it has made them repent and realize the need to embark on a new life, a life of prayer and reconciliation.'

'Yes,' I admitted, 'but perhaps under false pretences.'

'But grace often works in mysterious ways.'

He slumped back in his chair. The role of the apostate surrounded by the blind faithful was taking its toll. He looked exhausted, and I gently told him so.

'I'm not just exhausted,' he replied, almost in a whisper. 'If I don't get out of here, I think I shall go mad.'

He longed for nothing so much as to return to the green hills of Galilee, the hills where He walked.

In the evening, the power failed, and wasn't fully restored for my remaining week in Medjugorje. Never had I been quite so cold. I spent the days walking the hills surrounding the valley, attending mass, and praying. At night, I crawled into bed beneath a heap of blankets and read mystical poetry by Saint John of the Cross, Gerard Manley Hopkins and Saint Teresa of Avila in golden, flickering candlelight as the wind roared outside and hissed through the cracks in the walls. On Saint Teresa's book-plate was a laconic prayer:

> Let nothing disturb thee
> Nothing affright thee.
> All things are passing,
> God never changeth.
> Patient endurance
> Attaineth to all things.
> Who God possesseth
> In nothing is wanting,
> Alone God sufficeth.

I tried to see the visionaries, but Vicka's door remained closed, and her mail unanswered. I did meet up with Ivan, but when I mentioned that I was writing a book and was particularly keen to know more about the secrets, a look of undisguised terror crossed his face, and he fled. The other seers were all travelling, spreading the Medjugorje message.

I did, however, speak briefly with Father Slavko Barbarić, OFM, one of Medjugorje's most tireless propagandists and something of a mediator between the visionaries and the masses. This astute Franciscan theologian had initially been sent to Medjugorje by Pavao Zanić, Bishop of Mostar (and a sceptic of the apparitions) to uncover the 'hoax'. The Bishop's plot failed when Father Barbarić became a staunch supporter of the visionaries.

He claimed to know nothing of the contents of the ten secrets, but he did offer a metaphor: 'If you are driving along a road and suddenly you encounter a sign which reads "Caution, Deadly Danger Ahead!", that is not to say that you are about to die, but rather that you must pay special attention, or you could have a fatal accident. Your salvation depends upon you as well. If you convert, then perhaps the catastrophes of the secrets will appear less catastrophic.'

We were standing outside the rectory. There was something about Father Barbarić's voice which struck me as familiar. And then he reached into his robe to take out a cigarette, and I knew at once that we had met before. This was the Franciscan whom I had startled on my first hapless night in Medjugorje, the one who had denied me shelter on Christmas morning. Suddenly, he seemed to realize it too. It was an excruciating moment. I thanked him for his time and left, even more disappointed than after our first encounter.

As I walked across the esplanade in front of St James's, it began to snow. The wind blew in great gusts, barely giving the flakes a chance to touch ground. Along the main street, vendors of Virgin memorabilia were frantically packing up their wares; a group of boisterous Italian pilgrims were jostling to get on their bus, destination Bergamo; and some young toughs were screeching up and down the street in a late-model B M W, the radio throbbing bad Slavic rock and roll. Along a retaining wall at a building site, someone had scrawled some fresh graffito: 'UN: the Muslims are *not* our brothers!' I sought refuge in a café.

All of the patrons were foreign pilgrims, and I was instantly treated to the sort of effusive courtesy displayed by fellow travellers caught in a storm in a remote (although not evidently godforsaken) place. The altogether unique gathering consisted of a former child actor from Beverly Hills, an Irish beauty from Cork, a wizened Franciscan from Rome, a grain salesman from New Mexico, and a wheelchair-bound Pole who had volunteered for the Croatian army in the 'crusade against the Muslim horde', and had lost both legs when he stepped on a landmine outside Mostar. They all believed unconditionally in the miracles of Medjugorje.

It was hard not to take an interest in the conversation, since the decidedly vital topic was the end, as in the Apocalypse. The signs, everyone seemed to agree, were clear, and they attributed a prophetic character to, among other natural and human disasters: the AIDS and Ebola viruses, the deterioration of the ozone, the wild shift in weather patterns, the fall of communism (always a favourite), and the recently concluded local war.

I asked somewhat light-heartedly if they thought the end would come in a matter of days, weeks, or months.

The Pole grimly said 'Soon,' to which the others all nodded ponderously.

The child actor added that he had 'purposely, like, not bought a return ticket to LA'.

'In the Scripture,' I offered, '"soon" often meant thousands of years, or never. People have been waiting for the Apocalypse for two millennia.'

'You haven't been listening to the messages of Our Lady,' snapped the Irish beauty.

'Oh, but I have. I'm just not at all sure that they are truly her words.'

That was it. I had uttered heresy. Heads shook in disbelief. Backs turned in dissent. There was muttering. Only the grain salesman took pity, and thought he might still convince me. He produced an enlarged photograph which he had taken on Apparition Hill. 'Look,' he insisted earnestly, 'here is the proof, here is Our Lady as she appeared to me. Can't you see her?'

I gazed at the picture for a long time, but all I could see was the image of a sky at dusk in which innumerable rays of light were streaking through diaphanous clouds of mauve and pink. The truth was, it was a miraculous sky. A sky as only God could have made.

2 / Meeting Mother Ganges

Yadahareva virajet, tadahareva pravrajet.
(On the day on which he renounces, on that very day let him sally forth.)
   Agehananda Bharati

I walked into Gangotri in a failing light and a driving snow which obscured the surrounding peaks of the Garhwal Himalayas and reduced the Ganges river snaking through the gorge below to a low, scarcely audible murmur. The road was lined with buses and cars, silent and pristine beneath the snow. The thin mountain air was tinged with wood smoke and pine. As I approached a makeshift teashop, a canvas sheet which hung at the threshold was parted and a sinewy copper-coloured hand waved me out of the blinding storm and into the darkness. I stooped and entered beneath a cardboard sign which an unsure hand had scrawled with the ambitious title: *Holliday Hotel*.

Namaste, I offered, and the traditional greeting was repeated tenfold or more by a crowd that was little more than a collusion of shadows. The air was ripe with the smell of wet wool, fetid breath, aromatic tea, and a hint of hashish. A space was made for me before the fire, and I was handed a cup of sweet, milky tea.

As my eyes grew accustomed to the darkness, I made out a host of ochre-robed *sadhus*, or Hindu ascetics, interspersed among a gathering of merchants, drivers, porters, and pilgrims. They were waiting for the storm to pass to journey south, down the river valley to Uttarkashi, Dehra Dun, Rishikesh, and Hardwar. It was the third week in October; in just a few days, the road would close for the winter, and Gangotri, the site revered as the spiritual source of the sacred Ganges, would be home to only a handful of the most indurate holy men. I was, it seemed, travelling in the wrong direction.

Gangotri was only the first stop on my journey from the source of the Ganges to the supremely holy city of Varanasi some 500 miles to the south. By following the river, paying my respects at various stations of pilgrimage along its course, and observing the faithful as they worked, prayed, and made offerings to the Ganges, I hoped to penetrate what has always been for me the strangest and most inaccessible of the world religions.

I left my 'companions' at the *Holliday* and went off in search of more seemly lodging.

From the middle of a cantilever bridge which spanned the Ganges, I looked out at an array of ashrams, monasteries, *dharamshalas*, shops, and guest houses which encrusted the slopes on both sides of the river. The temple enshrining the goddess Ganga stood on the left bank. Built in the early eighteenth century by the Gurkha general Amar Sirgh Thapa, the sanctuary is, by Hindu temple standards, modest. A central, rectangular tower or *shikhara*, its gilded finial-capped cupola hidden beneath the snow, was surrounded by four diminutive replicas. A ghat (from the Sanskrit *ghatta*, 'a landing place' or 'steps on a riverside') led down to the water's edge. Blue strata of smoke rose from the temple compound and from a single ashram on the opposite bank. All the other buildings were shuttered. I made for the ashram invoking admittedly hollow prayers to the goddess Ganga in the hope that I wouldn't be turned away.

An ochre-robed figure was framed in the door. As I got closer, I could see that his face was etched with a blissful smile. At once, I knew I would be safe. I gladly bent to touch his feet, a traditional show of respect to an ascetic.

His name was Swami Sooroopananda. Wild, uncropped black

hair and a beard framed a face of taut brown skin and a beak of a nose. His eyes were black and messianic, and his robe did little to hide a skeletal frame. He was a devotee of Krishna, the second most venerated avatar in the Hindu pantheon after Rama, and a hero of arms rather than contemplation. Not that the Swami was the least bit bellicose. On the contrary, he appeared the picture of peace. But for his robes, beads, sandals and shawl, a framed photograph of his late guru, the indispensable sacred texts, and the most rudimentary kitchen utensils, he possessed nothing. His life was an example of asceticism.

He knew nothing of the world outside and, what's more, didn't care. His was a wind-swept and star-filled spiritual existence.

We sat by the open fire in his cinder-block dwelling, no more than ten metres square, and spoke of Gangotri, the Ganges, desire, and renunciation. I did not question him about his family or his past. Once a person becomes a *sadhu*, and dons the ochre robe, they renounce worldly desires and duties, caste and family. They undergo a symbolic cremation and become, in a ritualistic sense, a dead person walking.

I asked him if, as a non-Hindu, the sacred waters of the Ganges had the power to rid me of sin and purify my soul.

For a long while he was silent, and only stroked his beard in the glow of the firelight. I even thought that perhaps he hadn't heard me, or had simply ignored the question. Then he said: 'You are not born of a caste and so you cannot become a Hindu, at least not in an orthodox sense.' Again he paused. 'But *Ganga Ma* (Mother Ganges) is pure and holy. Take her waters. Meditate. I can tell you no more.'

In fact, it was a loaded question. I wasn't necessarily looking for redemption on the Ganges, but rather for a modest insight into the rites and rituals of the world's oldest religion in the hopes that they might lead me, however circuitously, to a

deeper understanding of my own tentative and doubt-filled faith.
I had not come to India having rejected my own religious–
spiritual traditions and looking for an alternative. I certainly did
not believe, as have so many seekers over the last few decades
fresh back from the subcontinent, that India is in any way nearer
the truth than many other parts of the world, or that India is
utterly spiritual and the West decadent. I did, however, believe
that there was value to be extracted from India, and the process
did not involve aping the locals. To immerse myself in the
Ganges would be of no more spiritual merit than, say, for Swami
Sooroopananda to take communion at St Peter's in the Vatican.

A riot of bells and gongs sounded from the temple across the
river calling the Hindu faithful to the evening service known as
arati. It was still snowing. In the twilight I followed the Swami, a
brisk flutter of ochre in a white whirlwind.

An ancient Brahman priest conducted the ceremony. He was
praying and offering sweets, fruit and marigolds to a small effigy
of the goddess Ganga on the ghat at the river's edge. The goddess bore a lotus flower in one hand and a vessel of water in the
other. As if on cue, the storm ceased. Some young attendants lit
incense and sandalwood. Apart from the temple priests and
attendants, the odd ascetic, and the Swami and myself, the only
others present were a Bengali pilgrim and his two teenage sons,
both of whom appeared exceedingly bored, as if they had seen it
all before. They kept looking my way in the hope, I thought, of
receiving a conspiratorial glance confirming that the ritual was
just so much arcane nonsense. It wasn't. The scene was full of
hints and signs of the numinous, however indecipherable. I was
spellbound. After a series of chants and finger gestures by the
priest, the whole congregation struck up a hymn, high-pitched
and unmelodious (at least to a Western ear). The priest then lit
an oil lamp with five flickering flames and revolved it around the

image of the goddess. The attendants began striking a gong, ringing bells and cymbals, and beating a drum. The music picked up pace, grew to a climax, and came to a halt in final, perfectly orchestrated accord.

The *arati* ended. The priest distributed sweets to the congregation. The *sadhus* shuffled away. The attendants packed up their instruments, and the teenage boys puffed on Marlboros and stamped their feet impatiently while their father lit an oil lamp, placed it in a paper boat, and set it afloat on the river. The vessel bobbed and circled at the water's edge until it was swept up by the current. After a brief voyage, it was swallowed up and extinguished by the sacred river.

I lingered at the temple. Darkness had fallen and the compound was illuminated by a combination of weak electric light provided by a raucous generator, and a silent constellation of oil lamps and votive candles. A number of stark cells opened on to the temple courtyard. They were occupied by ancient men, stooped and withered, but with the air of sages who were living out their last days and fulfilling the most profound desire of every devout Hindu: to die in sight of, or better still, immersed in, the Ganges. To do so is enough to achieve *mukti* or *moksa*, the release from the endless chain of birth, death, and rebirth known as *samsara*.

I looked into one of the cells and saw a figure reading Vedic verses in a sepulchral light. But for a simple bed and a private altar to Shiva, the cell was utterly bare. One of the young temple attendants approached me and whispered without preamble: 'Is famous professor from Delhi, will die soon.' All told, it didn't seem to me such a bad way to go.

Coming out of the temple after having gazed at the ferocious silver image of the goddess Ganga, I promptly stumbled over one of the most sacred stones in the Hindu cosmic geography, the Bhagiratha Shiva. To the uninitiated, the slab is as seemingly inconsequential as, say, the Stone of Unction in the Holy Sepulchre in Jerusalem. Its significance, however, is sublime. The tale goes like this:

In the seminal Indian epic the Ramayana, a sage recounts the penance, or *tapa*, undertaken by the king Bhagiratha in order to bring the celestial Ganga to earth so that her purifying waters might redeem the accursed souls of 60,000 of his dissolute forebears who had been reduced to ashes for having mocked a holy man. (In India, reverence for holy men is the result of genuine piety, and not a small dose of fear.) For a full year or several centuries (accounts vary), Bhagiratha stood on tiptoe with his arms outstretched, renouncing both sustenance and support. The king's toil wasn't in vain. The Ganga was released from her heavenly abode, but so as to break her fall, Shiva (whose abode is the Himalayas) caught the torrent on his brow and let the water flow through the locks of his hair. The river descended to earth in seven streams, the *Saptasindhava*, of which the Ganges is one, although along the upper reaches the river is still known as the Bhagiratha.

In both Hindi and Urdu and a host of Indian languages, a 'Bhagiratha-like effort' is one which is undertaken against insurmountable odds, rather like the labours of Sisyphus, only in this case Bhagiratha's austerities were rewarded and the 60,000 souls resurrected.

A woman was huddled by the fire when I returned to the ashram. The flames highlighted her auburn hair and revealed a face of hollow cheeks and plaintive eyes. The Swami introduced her as Karen, although she immediately insisted on being called Chandika after the guardian-goddess and one of the multiple incarnations of Devi.

'What's the matter with Karen?' I asked.

'It's a name from another life,' she replied rather affectedly.

She had come up from Lucknow with no particular itinerary or destination. Her guru, to whom she had tirelessly dedicated the last three years of her life, had died. She had been at his side until the end.

'No one was so close to him as I was,' she offered.

'How many others were there?' I asked.

'Before he got ill, hundreds. In the end, only me.'

Now her guru was dead, his body reduced to ash, and his soul, no doubt, in complete accord with the absolute or Brahman. Karen-Chandika, however, was alone and hadn't the vaguest idea what to do. She let drop a number of hints that perhaps she would stay on in Gangotri. The Swami rocked on his heels, shook his head ambiguously, and stared silently at the fire. I didn't think he fancied her company or the prospect of another mouth to feed through a long burdensome Himalayan winter. He was no guru, but an ascetic. Nor did he appear to be looking for followers.

'Rishikesh might be a nice place to pass the winter,' I said, referring to the town downstream which is something of a haven for gurus and Western seekers alike.

'Yes!' agreed the Swami.

Now it was Karen-Chandika who stared silently at the fire.

I rose and said good night. Outside, the wind blew up great, billowing clouds of snow and caused the monumental deodars to sway and creak. I retired to my cell and drifted off to sleep to the steady lullaby of the Ganges.

At dawn, I walked down to the river to wash. Gangotri lay silent and undefiled beneath a blanket of snow. The sun would not rise over the eastern slope of the valley for hours and the chill of the night still clung to the village, but the sky was clear and full of stars. Suspended above a crag hung a pale sickle moon. The storm had passed.

The water was painfully cold. I washed rather timidly and did my best not to shriek. On the opposite bank, a priest was clearly made of better stuff; he was serenely standing knee-deep and bare-chested in the frigid current, taking up the water in his cupped hands, letting it run through his fingers in libation, and reciting a prescribed prayer to the Seven Sacred Rivers:

Gange cha! Yamune chaiva!
Godavari! Saraswati!
Narmade! Sindhu! Kaveri!
Jale asmin sannidhim kuru.

(O, Ganga! O, Yamuna!
O, Godavari! O, Saraswati!
O, Narmada, Sindhu, Kaveri!
May you all be pleased to be manifest in these waters!)

The priest emerged from his ritualistic bath supposedly pure and free of sin. After a bit of tentative splashing, I, as a non-Hindu, came away only marginally cleaner and numbly refreshed.

After a breakfast of tea and unleavened bread, I set off for the Gangotri Glacier, the physical source of the Ganges. The Swami looked concerned when I departed, but he had given me his blessing, an apple, and a small bottle to fill with the water that emerges pure and untainted from the ice cave known as Gomukh, the 'Cow's Mouth', located at the foot of the glacier.

It was a twelve-mile hike up-valley and, if the weather held, I expected to pass the night in the hamlet of Bhojbasa and reach the glacier the following morning.

The track cut into the slope above the river and had been worn smooth over the centuries by an incalculable multitude of pilgrims. By late morning, the sun was high in a cerulean-blue sky and had melted all but a few shade-filled patches of snow. The Ganges glistened. I came to a forest of deodars, larches and pines, a few rhododendron, and a solitary birch. As I emerged from the trees, I was confronted with the triad of peaks known as the Bhagirathi Sisters, all of which soar to more than 20,000 feet. I spent the better part of an hour simply gazing at the scene. In the unsullied Himalayan air, the landscape was as flawless as finely etched crystal. In a high-altitude pasture, I thought I could make out blue sheep.

Not a soul came up the track, but a number of young porters came down. They couldn't have been more than twelve or fourteen years old, but on their stooped backs they carried enormous burlap bundles full of blankets, pots and pans, tools, and other miscellaneous gear from the tea or *chai* shops that cater to pilgrims and trekkers. Winter was fast approaching and they were headed down-valley to their families in Uttarkashi. Their shoes were riddled with holes and their clothes were little more than rags. They had the distant, resigned look of beasts of burden. I gave them chocolate, but what they really wanted were my cigarettes. When I relented, they smiled, revealing swollen gums and rotting teeth.

As the afternoon progressed, I began to feel ill. I had an excruciating headache and dizzy spells. At close to 13,000 feet, the air was thin, and I knew at once that I was suffering from altitude sickness. The cure was simple: descend. But I wasn't about to turn around when I was so near to my destination. I cursed myself for not having taken the time to acclimatize properly. My pace slowed to a shuffle, and in the late afternoon I stumbled into Bhojbasa, my head reeling.

The hamlet lay in the centre of a singularly desolate valley. There wasn't a tree in sight. I made for the ashram of Lal Baba, a 'holy man' who, I later discovered, had single-handedly deforested the valley, and possessed a fondness for young male trekkers and unsuspecting pilgrims. I found him ensconced in an armchair in front of his ashram surrounded by servants and panderers. He wore impossibly thick glasses which hid his eyes, a greasy woollen shawl and bedroom slippers. There was scarcely a tooth in his aged head. He beckoned me to sit by his side, and then proceeded to pat my knee. I shifted. An obsequious underling produced a book of receipts for the 'voluntary' donation to the ashram. They asked for a sum which, relative to India, was astronomical. I baulked, but was in no mood to haggle so I paid up. Although the ashram consisted of a number of modest bungalows, I was led to a trap door at the edge of the compound and shown a dank, subterranean chamber of unspeakable seediness. When I protested, Lal Baba responded unequivocally: '*You* may come and sleep with me!' His entourage howled with laughter. I stomped off in a fury.

I walked up the hill to a government-run shelter and found a team of porters smoking around a fire of rags soaked in kerosene. It was a cheerless scene, but then government-run shelters are not renowned for their cheeriness. I slept alone in a dormitory, but it was a fitful sleep; my head pounded relentlessly, and over my sleeping bag pattered a steady succession of rats.

At sunrise, I was standing at the river's edge watching the first rays of light illuminate the ragged, pyramidic summit of Shiv Ling peak, and slowly descend to reveal the azure colossus of the Gangotri Glacier. I felt as if I were witnessing the dawn of creation. Suddenly, the previously impenetrable notions which govern the Hindu universe – the illusory nature of phenomenal experience, the transmigration of souls, the Brahman or absolute spirit as a conjunction of being, consciousness, and bliss – didn't seem so arcane. For a moment, I dwelt in a dimension prescribed by fundamentally distinct laws, and my world and all its parameters seemed a universe away. For that brief and fleeting insight alone, I was glad I had come.

As I approached the Cow's Mouth, the cave at the foot of the glacier from which the Ganges springs, I saw that I was not alone. A *sadhu* stood in the first pool which formed at the river's source, precisely where a landscape painter would have positioned him to give the glacier scale. He was in the midst of his morning ablutions. I kept my distance so as not to disturb the ritual. When he finished his bath, he climbed atop a boulder in the river and sat in a meditative pose.

The water was flowing out of the Cow's Mouth with terrific force, but here at the headwaters, the Ganges was no more than fifty feet wide at best. True, the Ganges would be joined by scores of other rivers along its 1,560-mile course, but still, it was hard to believe that this was the actual source of the mighty river that wound its way across north-east India before spilling out into innumerable streams, rivulets and estuaries and into the Bay of Bengal. For untold millions of Hindus, this was the river in which, or with whose waters, they bathed, drank, watered their livestock, washed their clothes, irrigated their fields, performed their rites, and scattered the ashes of their dead. Nevertheless, it looked somehow insubstantial.

Given that, in all likelihood, I would never again find myself at the source of the Ganges, and at the same time rather ashamed of my craven attempt at a bath in Gangotri, I stripped and plunged into the river. Not a knee-deep dip, mind you, but a full immersion. The experience brought me as near to the sensation of a full-blown cardiac arrest as I think I have ever been. I shot out of the water like a man possessed. As I stood quaking at the riverside, the *sadhu*, I noticed, hadn't moved a muscle, except the one that brought on a slight but unmistakable smile.

I spent the day reading Hindu mythology; basking in the Himalayan sun; and trying my best to coax my limbs into a semblance of yogic positions.

The Bengali and his despondent sons were checking into the shelter at Bhojbasa when I arrived back at dusk. Although we hadn't exchanged a word at Gangotri, the father appeared elated to see me. We sat on the veranda in the diminishing light. Again the weather was changing and the sky grew heavy with the threat of more snow. The magnificent peaks disappeared.

For years, he explained, he had dreamed of taking his sons to one of the most hallowed sites in the Hindu world, and now, on the verge of fulfilling his long-awaited desire, his sons were indifferent, hostile even, to the whole enterprise. They hardly spoke. Having two sons myself, I silently hoped, futilely perhaps, that I would never find myself in a similar situation.

'In the years to come, they will thank you,' I said.

'And what good does that do me now?'

'Very little, I suppose, but I'm sure they will never forget this journey.'

'They think only of the West; their clothes, their music, their opinions are all polluted by foreign ideas!'

'When they find themselves at the source, maybe they'll have a change of heart. I found the experience to be transcendental.'

'*You* have no idea what it *really* feels like to make it here.'

True enough, I thought, but I objected to his inflections. What's more, he was beginning to fix me with a stare of undisguised contempt, as if I were the personification of the West and the corruptor of his offspring.

'And how does it *really* feel to make it here?' I asked.

'You wouldn't understand.'

'Try me.'

But he didn't. He looked away and said nothing. I had encountered a few like him during this journey and others to India. To him, I was a *mleccha*, a Sanskrit word used to identify a barbarian, or indeed anyone born outside of India which, to men like these, were one and the same. A good many Hindus exhibit a form of cultural schizophrenia towards the West. They admire the technical achievements of the highly industrialized world, but they deplore the excessive materialism of Western societies and their supposed lack of spiritual values. The West, they often claim, has knowledge, but India possesses wisdom.

I didn't think it was quite so simple, or the division so clear-cut.

He noticed that among my maps and notebooks was a copy of the Upanishad, one of the canonical texts of Hinduism.

'To discover true spirituality, you from the West must come to India. There is the proof. What have you produced which could possibly compare to the Upanishad?'

'Have you ever read the Bible?' I asked, taking a rather liberal geographical view of the West to encompass anything west of the Arabian Sea. 'The Song of Solomon, the Gospels, or the Epistles? Have you read the Talmud?'

Silence.

'How about Plato, Aristotle, Boethius, Aquinas, Plotinus, Seneca, Vico, Emerson, Thoreau, or Nietzsche?'

'No,' he replied, 'but *our* literature is much older!'

'If what you are saying is that what is old in religion or philosophy is better, then you must regard animism as particularly sacred. To me antiquity is no claim to anything. I have discovered great wisdom in the Upanishad,' I said, 'just as I have in many sacred texts – the Koran, for instance.'

This last declaration had its desired effect. He fled.

No sooner had the Bengali left, however, than I made out a solitary figure walking towards the shelter. It was Karen-Chandika.

★

In the evening, the cook stood before the table, bowed his head, and with his lower lip quivering, announced that there was no food. The porters berated him in the local Garhwali dialect and, I gathered, accused him of hoarding provisions. The cook produced a decidedly substantial kitchen knife and wielded it threateningly at his accusers. A certain calm descended when I produced four packets of dry *tallarines al pesto*. Everyone ate except the Bengali, who suspected the dish, although clearly vegetarian, of somehow not being high-Hindu fare. I think it was the eggs in the pasta. His sons, however, were delighted. They immediately associated my munificence with pasta with more ambitious wealth.

'You are businessman with industry or company perhaps?' one asked.

'No, I'm afraid not.'

'We will run your computer department,' said the other.

'I have no computer department.'

'Bill Gates says Indians are the second most intelligent people on earth,' proclaimed the first.

'He would know. And who would the first be?'

'Chinese,' they replied. 'Know why?'

'No.'

And then one of them squinted his eyes and said, 'The abacus, it's the world's first computer.'

Throughout dinner, Karen-Chandika was morose, or else she was trying to cultivate an air of Eastern resignation and calm. She hardly uttered a word. When almost everyone else had retired, however, she drew her chair nearer and adopted a grave tone.

'I have a very special favour to ask of you,' she said.

'Yes?'

'I would like you to bring something to Swami Sooroopan-anda for me.'

'What exactly?'

'The ashes of my late guru.'

'The what!?'

'They are very blessed.'

'No doubt, but why do you need me to deliver your guru's re-mains? You too have to pass through Gangotri when you descend.'

'Not all his ashes, just a small vessel.'

'It's not the quantity that concerns me.'

She proceeded to reach into her shoulder bag and produce a diminutive brass urn. She placed it on the table and pushed it towards me. I squirmed in my chair.

'I'm not sure I will have time to see the Swami when I return to Gangotri. You would be doing me a tremendous favour,' she pleaded.

This was rubbish. The ashram was no more than a two-minute walk from the trail along which she would have to pass on the way down. It must have ended badly between her and the Swami. He must have kicked her out.

'Very well,' I said. But I immediately began to have reserva-tions. What if I dropped the urn? Or the contents spilled out in my backpack and my clothes and belongings became impreg-nated with the ashes of some guru whom I not only didn't revere, but didn't even know? What if the Swami wouldn't accept them, what then?

'But what if . . .'

'A *tremendous* favour,' she insisted.

When I passed the ashes to the Swami as we sat before the fire the following evening in Gangotri, he took the urn with a shrug. Of Karen-Chandika he didn't want to hear a word.

In the morning it was snowing again. I left the Swami as he readied his shelter for the Himalayan winter and six months of solitude.

★

God First,

World Second,

Self Last.

    (Road sign on the outskirts of Hardwar)

At Hardwar, the Ganges emerges from the Himalayan foothills,
spills into the North Indian Plain, and begins its long, sluggish
course southeast to the Bay of Bengal.

The devotees of Shiva call the city *har-dwar*, the 'Gate of
Shiva'. Those who revere Vishnu pronounce the name as *hari-
dwar*, the 'Gate of Vishnu'. The less sectarian simply refer to the
city as the 'Gate of God'. Hardwar is a monastic centre and a pilgrimage site of the first order. The faithful flock here because Hardwar is a *tirtha*, a spiritual 'ford' or 'crossing place' where heaven
and earth meet. It is a highly charged sacred terrain which is conceived of as a threshold between 'this shore' and the 'far shore'.
For Hindus, prayers or offerings are meritorious anywhere, but
especially so at a *tirtha*, where the divine is more readily accessible.
The Hindu sacred geography is replete with *tirthas* including
Hardwar, Varanasi, Mathura, Ayodhya, and the Prayag which
marks the confluence of the Ganges and the Yamuna rivers.

At Hardwar, religious sanctions are no light matter, as a notice
at the train station made clear: 'WARNING! In the muni-
cipality of Hardwar, meat, eggs, fish, alcoholic drink, wine, drugs
(charas, ganja, bang, opium, heroine [*sic*]) are forbidden and will
lead to jail and fine and expulsion!' Still, eggs could be furtively
procured, I was told by a daring merchant, 'for a price'.

I checked into a guest house near the ghats that was run by an
elderly Brahman couple with impeccable manners and an inveter-
ate admiration for all things British. My room was done up in
faded chintz, and on the walls hung sepia photographs of the
British at play in the Raj (never mind that Indians, Brahman
or otherwise, were resolutely barred from many such scenes,

except, of course, in the role of servants). After the austerity of my cell in Gangotri, and the rodent-infested shelter at Bhojbasa, I felt as if I were a maharajah in his palace.

I strolled along the riverfront in the fine early-morning light in the direction of the Har-ki-pairi, the 'steps of the Lord', also known as the Brahmakund or 'pond of Brahma', an expanse of water along the Ganges that is the sanctum sanctorum of Hardwar. The promenade was teeming. In addition to the habitual merchants, and the young boys strolling hand in hand, the hollow-eyed urchins and desperate, mutilated beggars, the sea of sari-clad women and spotless, uniformed schoolgirls, and, naturally, the sacred, listless Brahman cows and the shrewd, ill-tempered monkeys, I was struck by the sheer quantity of religious figures. I passed *sadhus* and monks draped in ochre, yellow, white and vermilion robes, and more regally clad *mahants*, bearded and wreathed with garlands of marigolds. There were female *sadhus* too, and nearly naked *naga sadhus*, their bodies smeared with ashes and their hair an anarchy of matted locks. There were child *sadhus*, and trident-bearing *sadhus*, and others blowing on conch shells, or meditating amidst the chaos, or taking long, lung-collapsing tokes on *chillum* pipes packed with bang. I felt as if I had alighted in another world, in another age. Here, it was the *sadhus* who represented convention; I was indisputably the odd man out.

At the entrance to the Har-ki-pairi, a sign reminded visitors that the sacred precinct was off-limits to non-Hindus, but I took advantage of the throng and ignored the injunction. I wanted to see the footprints of Vishnu set in stone which are a singular object of awe for Hindus. This was, after all, the deity who crossed the seven regions of the Hindu universe in three effortless strides. When I approached the relic, however, a custodian promptly pulled a curtain across the slab and demanded a twenty-*rupee* fee. I payed grudgingly, but the imprints were rather a letdown; no less so, it should be said, than the footprints of the Prophet Mohammed or the handprint of the archangel Gabriel in the Qubbat el-Sakhra in Jerusalem. All are fruits, in my opinion, of hoary imaginations seeking a tangible object to square with myth.

Sitting on the steps of the ghat, I felt a bit of a voyeur. Hindu men and boys (women bathed farther upstream) were doffing their *dhotis*, the long piece of cotton draped around the waist and tugged between the legs, and were left only in a kind of G-string known as a *kaupina*. The colour of their skin varied considerably, from the ebony of some south Indians to the pallid white frames of the Kashmiris. Although the water was less frigid than at the foot of the Gangotri Glacier, it was still numbingly cold, but I didn't see a soul testing the waters with a feeble toe. They all descended the steps and entered the water with an admirable resolve. Some dunked up and down with an athletic air; others clung to chains that were strung along the water's edge so as not to be swept away by the current; while still others did just that, floating downstream to some unknown landing place.

There came a tap on my shoulder. I turned to find an elderly and severe-looking *panda*, one of the temple priests whose function it is to guide and administer to pilgrims in their ritualistic observances.

'Out,' he said laconically, and proceeded to show me the way.

I followed meekly, feeling like a party crasher. All eyes were turned on me, the intruder, the *mleccha*, the creature lower than the lowest caste because I had no caste.

I wandered the riverbank and came upon the more accommodating Kusha Ghat where no prohibitions applied. In addition to ritualistic bathing, a good many of the people were involved in more mundane chores: washing laundry, gossiping, sitting idly, or perusing the newspaper. In a sense, the ghat serves the same function as a city or village square in the

Mediterranean world; it is a place of social interaction and communication. It is a stage.

An elderly, sage-looking *sadhu* sitting just below me at the ghat was mumbling ancient verses from a tome. I must have given him the unnerving sensation of reading over his shoulder, because suddenly he closed the book with a clap, wheeled around, and invited me to join him.

'What is troubling you?' he asked in flawless English.

'It seems I am ritualistically polluted,' I said.

'You have been barred from the Har-ki-pairi?'

'I have.'

'The *pandas*, they are very narrow-minded fellows. Do not take it to heart. Here too we are beholding *Ganga*.'

But I persisted. 'Was the motive for my being excluded from the Har-ki-pairi based on any scriptural dictate?'

'No, it is tradition, that is all. You are not a Hindu and for the *pandas* that is enough.'

That was the crux of it. Hinduism, like Judaism, is a national rather than a universal faith. One may choose to become a Christian, a Muslim, a Buddhist, or a Shamanist, but one cannot become a Hindu (or a Jew), at least not in a manner recognized by the orthodoxy. It is a question of birth. That is why Hindus do not go about proselytizing (the Hari Krishna sect is an aberration). There has never existed any sort of call to conversion, no injunction equivalent to Christ saying, 'Go ye into all lands.'

'It seems a bit unfair,' I said. 'I am forever being told of India's exalted spirituality, of her millennia-old wisdom, yet if one should try to embrace it, the *panda* and the priest say "out!"'

'Our wisdom is there to be grasped, but not so all of our rituals. People must not abandon their faith. All religions seek the truth: "There is only one truth, but Wise Men call it by many names."'

I recognized this ecumenical-sounding axiom from the

Upanishad, but I found it misleading at best, and under close scrutiny, wholly naïve. To begin with, those words were pronounced and later recorded when Hinduism reigned undisputed by either Buddhism or Jainism, and obviously, Christianity and Islam as well. Furthermore, I did not regard all religions as inherently the same; worthy of respect yes, but the same no. Jews, Hindus, Muslims and Christians all subscribe to an all-powerful Being in all eternity. Jainism is radically atheistic; and the Buddha explicitly rejected the notion of an Absolute Being. The manner in which Jews, Muslims, Hindus, and Christians conceive of the universe as a static entity is diametrically opposed to that of the Buddhist, who views the universe as in perpetual flux. The difference can be summed up in the age-old philosophical division between being and becoming.

'Ah! Right you are,' said the *sadhu*, laughing nervously.

In fact, I had the distinct impression that he hadn't the slightest notion of comparative religion. The idea of studying other sacred texts, or taking an interest in other faiths, very probably had never entered his head. He was blissfully happy in his Brahman-inspired universe. I, for one, could hardly blame him.

'And now I must get back to my verses. Come and see me again tomorrow,' he said, pushing up his pince-nez and burying his face where he had left off in the ancient Sanskrit text.

But I didn't see him again. At Hardwar, I had found the 'Gate of God' ajar, but when I approached, it was firmly shut. Now I was off to other sacred sites, hoping all the while to find an open door.

It had been my intention to take a rowboat from Hardwar to Varanasi, and to observe, from an intimate and privileged vantage point, the rhythms and rituals of life along the Ganges. But it was, I discovered, an ill-conceived plan. I had been reading Eric Newby's classic *Slowly Down the Ganges*, and his account of the boat journey south of Hardwar reads like a cautionary tale. He and his party ran aground in the shallow, rock-strewn and shoal-filled waters a full thirty-five times between Hardwar and the Balawali bridge, a distance of no more than twenty miles. I was intent on drifting, not pushing, wading, and portaging.

I booked a train ticket to Allahabad.

The trip was to take eight hours, but in India, distances are seemingly interminable, and timetables are consulted exclusively by unsuspecting and well-intentioned foreigners. After twenty-two hours of sweltering, second-class hell, wedged between a spartan Sikh and a family of Punjabis who scarcely stopped eating the lavish picnic which they had wisely prepared for the journey, I arrived in Allahabad exhausted, feverish, and reeking of curry.

At Allahabad, the Ganges, the Yamuna and the mythical or long-since-dried-up Saraswati (no one is altogether sure) converge at a place known as the Prayag or the Sangam, both of which mean 'confluence', or the Triveni, the 'confluence of the three'. There is no more exalted bathing site in India. The Prayag is one of the 'great seven' pilgrimage sites or *saptamahatirtha*, along with Hardwar, Varanasi, Dwarka, Ayodhya, Mathura, and Ujjain, but even among these the Prayag is pre-eminent, often being called the *Tirth Raj* or 'king of all pilgrimage places'.

It is at the Prayag that every twelve years, when Jupiter is in Aquarius, devout Hindus gather for the Kumbh Mela, the single largest religious spectacle on earth. The astrological-astronomical moment is considered auspicious, and literally millions of pilgrims journey from all over the subcontinent and abroad to bathe at the confluence, make their offerings, visit shrines, and seek religious instruction and advice on matters sacred and profane from among the whole panoply of monks, *sadhus*, *mahants*, seers, saints and pandits. At the last Kumbh

Mela, in 1989, the number of pilgrims was said to be in the neighbourhood of ten million.

I took a bicycle rickshaw from the orderly Civil Lines district
built by the British to the Sangam about four miles outside town.
I was well off the habitual tourist route, and a great many of the
people driving past in cars or trucks or on motorcycles, riding in
rickshaws, or strolling beneath the avenues of tamarind, fig, and
magnolia trees, seemed genuinely astonished to see a West-
erner. They shouted greetings, honked horns, waved, or simply
stared. I felt rather too conspicuous in the open rickshaw, too
much the sahib. Some young boys on bicycles pedalled alongside
to strike up conversation and practise their English, asking variously: where was I from; if I was a coffee drinker; how many
sisters I had; and whether I preferred sandals or shoes. I replied
politely to these textbook questions and they veered off beaming
and triumphant.

The final approach to the Sangam is a vast wasteland, flat and
virtually treeless, where the pilgrims pitch their tents and set up
camp during the Kumbh Mela. Along the east bank of the
Yamuna, in the shadows of the battlements of the sprawling
sixteenth-century fort built by the Moghul emperor Akbar, stalls
sold rice, marigolds, coconuts, milk, and other offerings which
the pilgrims would cast into the river. There were barbers
shaving the heads and beards of male pilgrims before they took
their ritualistic dip. And pandits sat on makeshift daises listening
to the faithful and offering priestly counsel.

At the river's edge, a flotilla of brightly painted and canopied
boats waited to row the pilgrims to the sacred confluence. The
boatmen were jostling to take on the pilgrims, often insisting on
exorbitant fees knowing full well that they had the devout in
their palms, for there was no other way for the pilgrims to get to
their longed-for destination.

They saw me coming.

'Sahib! Sahib!' they shouted in a chorus, bowing obsequiously and grinning hustlers' grins.

For lack of any other criteria, I sought out the most cheerfully painted vessel and began to haggle the price of the half-mile journey down-river. The sum was absurdly high and the boatman refused to negotiate. Finally, I chose an old boatman who had remained silent at the edge of the crowd. I stated a reasonable price and stepped into his boat. Three other boatmen climbed aboard and off we rowed.

For anyone but the pious Hindu, the Sangam is a singularly uninteresting site. The muddy brown Ganges meets the vile green Yamuna and in the sickly-coloured confluence devotees stand waist-deep and perform their *puja*, or offering, under the watchful gaze of Brahman priests who assure that the ritual unfolds in the orthodox manner, and, incidentally, charge handsomely for their services. For the Hindu, however, it is an ecstatic moment, often the culmination of a lifelong aspiration. As I watched the pilgrims in the process of their immersions, their faces reflected unbounded and unmitigated rapture. My mind conjured up visions of ancient baptisms in the river Jordan.

I actually contemplated a dip, but the stench and the accumulated filth floating on the oily surface of the water made me think better of it.

On the return journey, I asked how long it would take to reach Varanasi by boat. The boatmen conferred. There was nodding, a bit of disagreement, some wild gesticulating. Then I heard the name Kashi, the 'city of light', the most ancient name for Varanasi. Finally, they agreed that it would take three to five days depending on the currents. 'And how much would they charge?' I asked, trying to appear merely curious. This second conference took slightly longer, during which time they each eyed me up and down to ascertain just what I might be worth. A high sum was mentioned, but I shook my head and pretended to abandon the idea. There came a second price, and then a third, the equivalent of about one hundred and fifty dollars, a small fortune in rural India, but certainly within my means. It wasn't just the five days downstream, they insisted; they would have to tow the boat back upstream, and that would take nearly two more weeks. Suddenly the price struck me as a pittance. I felt like the Great White Oppressor. I quoted a price just slightly higher. At first they looked puzzled; then we shook hands, and they appeared elated. So was I. We agreed to meet the following morning at first light.

When I appeared on the riverbank in the morning weighted down with provisions for the journey, I found the elderly boatman poised and ready, but gone was the smartly painted and sleek craft of the day before. Instead, I was ushered to a thoroughly decrepit vessel of dubious seaworthiness. The hull was unpainted and wore a patchwork of tin sheeting. The oars consisted of bamboo poles and pieces of scrap wood for blades. From the bow to the square, junk-like stern, the boat was no more than twenty feet long, and the beam probably measured less than five feet. The deck was covered with a thatched canopy supported by iron hoops over which was stretched a lurid yellow plastic tarp advertising a brand of Japanese batteries.

I protested; I threw up my hands; I kicked at the mud; I railed that this was *not* the boat that I had hired, and certainly not for the sum I had been quoted. I demanded that the boat from the previous day be found. I cursed heaven and hell. And then I looked into the quiet, resigned eyes of the boatman and realized that yesterday's boat was probably not even his, but likely belonged to some lazy *panda* who allowed him to ferry pilgrims to and fro, and break his back at the oars, and sweat beneath the ferocious sun for a miserable cut of the earnings. This boat, however, was his, and he had cleaned it up as best he could, and hung a series of flimsy, florid curtains from the canopy to protect me from the sun, and had found some tattered cushion God knows where so that Sahib could rest his white arse and float down *Ganga Ma* in relative comfort, and when we got to Varanasi, the money would be his, and he could feed his dozen children for a full six months.

And so I quietly boarded. Soon we were joined by one of the boatmen from the day before, and we pushed off from the muddy bank bound for Varanasi. It would be a journey of three to five days I was told; the distance was more difficult to calcu-late given the serpentine course of the Ganges. When I asked the boatmen how many miles separated the Prayag from Varanasi, they stared blankly; they had never heard of a mile.

They were half-brothers. Bola Nath, the elderly boatman or *nisad*, was black-skinned and had the limber, stick-like frame of a contortionist. Although he was seventy years old, his face hardly bore a wrinkle and his black eyes were clear and steady. He rarely spoke. His brother Amer Nath was fifty. His skin was the colour of rich brown tobacco. He was heavier than his brother and had sagging jowels and a soft, round belly. He was talkative, jovial, and, unlike Bola, knew some rudimentary English. Both men wore *dhotis*; they went barefoot; and around their necks hung amulets containing their mantras.

I liked them both.

As we rowed past the Sangam, the confluence was already crowded with pilgrims immersing themselves, chanting, and tossing their offerings into the swirling current. Women climbed out of the water on to platforms and their wet, brilliantly coloured saris clung to their bodies and showed off the rounded breasts and voluptuous hips that were like erotic temple carvings.

When we didn't stop at the confluence, Bola and Amer Nath's fellow boatmen called out and asked where we were going. 'To

Kashi,' they replied. And the boatmen waved, and hailed us, and bid us a safe journey; and slowly they drifted out of sight.

There was a steady current now, thanks to the added volume of water as the Yamuna joined the Ganges. Bola and Amer hardly had to row, except to keep the boat pointed downstream. There were whirlpools, and in places the yellow-tinged water bubbled and belched. To the right, the high sandbank obscured the landscape beyond. On the opposite shore, however, stretched an expansive, empty tract of sand and a far-off horizon of emerald-green trees. Occasionally, we passed women washing clothes in the river; or young boys bathing their herds of glistening water buffalo; or fishermen staking their net traps in mid-stream. The scene conformed precisely to how I had always imagined a journey down the Ganges would be.

In the afternoon, we passed a corpse, white and bloated, whirling in the current. It was a grisly, hard-to-dispel image, and I looked away in horror, but it was as integral a part of the river scene as the fishermen or the washerwomen. Bola and Amer looked on impassively. While it is true that the Hindus cremate their dead and cast the ashes upon the river, the corpses of *sadhus* and children, both of whom are considered pure and without sin, are simply deposited midstream. So too are many of the destitute, whose families can scarcely afford the high price of wood for a proper funeral pyre. I came to train my eyes on the surface of the river in an attempt to anticipate the grim debris.

We moored for the night along the right bank in the company of some fishermen. Amer went off in search of wood, but only managed to procure cow dung cakes, the principal fuel in rural India. We made a fire on the shore, and Bola prepared a dinner of *chapati* or unleavened bread; *sabji*, an incendiary vegetable curry made with potatoes, cauliflower, and chillies; and *dal*, a lentil dish that is the chief source of protein in the Hindu vegetarian diet.

After dinner, Bola and Amer filled a *chillum* pipe with bang and smoked contentedly; it was the sole moment of relaxation in a long day pulling at the oars. Seeing that there was no possibility of a brush with the law, I happily joined them.

Later, we fixed our beds on the boat. Bola and Amer lay side by side. There was a half moon and a warm breeze. From time to time, jackals shrieked from the dark bank, and Bola and Amer whispered and giggled. I took a long time falling off to sleep. I was as happy as I could remember.

There were still brilliant stars in the early morning sky when I awoke to the sound of hacking and spitting as Bola and Amer and dozens of fishermen and villagers took their morning bath. This wasn't their ritualistic bath, just a bath to get clean. For all the grime that one sees in India, people of every class and caste are meticulous in their bathing habits. I too washed in the river, but I couldn't help but think that with every splash I was covering myself with untold millions of amoebae which might carry hepatitis, amoebic dysentery, typhoid, and cholera. I resolved not to worry since there was little I could do.

We set off and landed on the opposite, uninhabited shore to relieve ourselves (to urinate or defecate in the river is considered an unspeakable sacrilege). As I walked out into the sandy expanse, I came upon human skulls and bones bleached white from the sun. I soon learned to step gingerly, but I never quite acquired the Indian gift of squatting gracefully.

When I returned to the boat, Bola and Amer were immersed in the river and their prayers. '*Gange cha! Yamune chaiva!* . . .' They were, in a ritualistic sense at least, a privileged pair, as were all the Hindus who lived and worked along the banks of the Ganges. They reminded me of the Jews and Christians of Jerusalem, or the Muslims of Mecca.

Bola seemed less pious than his brother, who would sometimes produce a prayer book in a comic-strip format and recite before dinner; but it was Bola who invariably sprinkled *Ganga* water on the bow of the boat before setting off. He had the superstitious streak of the sailor, and the captain's undivided love for his vessel.

When the sun reached its zenith in the white sky, the heat was infernal; the air came in hot bursts, and the Ganges seemed hardly to move. I rigged a makeshift canopy above the bow so that Bola and Amer could escape the direct sun. To this and every other gesture of simple consideration, from peeling them fruit and taking a turn at the oars, to offering them biscuits, vitamins, or tobacco, their initial reaction was invariably one of utter disbelief. For millions of low-caste Hindus (and I suspected that both Bola and Amer belonged to the lowest, *Shudra* caste), not to mention the Untouchables who are so debased as to be outside the caste system, Indian life can be a relentless series of blows, humiliations, and defeats great and small. It's not that I was attempting single-handedly to erase a lifetime of suffering. I did these things for Bola and Amer unconsciously. They were hard workers and worthy of respect. They were good to me. For all of India's millennia-old legacy of spirituality, I often found the country lacking in the most elemental humanity. I have heard countless Indians of the three 'twice-born' castes – Brahmans, Kshatriyas and Vaishyas – defend the caste system as the great unifying element that has kept Hindu society intact for centuries. Without the system, they say, there would be chaos. I cannot accept it. Let a Brahman, or better still one of his children, spend even a day as an Untouchable, or to use the euphemism coined by Gandhi, a *Harijan* or 'child of God', and then let him pronounce his defence of the inalienable system.

I found the slow, measured pace of the boat journey to be almost hypnotic in its effect. I wrote less than was customary, and read less still. Gazing out at the Ganges was entertainment enough. From time to time, dolphins leapt above the surface of the water quite close to the boat. I was astonished that they survived in these waters, because along certain reaches the pollution was thick and foul-smelling, a fact which did not prevent Bola and Amer from dipping their tin cups over the edge and drinking straight from the river. Had I followed their lead, I'm quite sure I wouldn't have survived a day.

The banks of the river presented contrasting scenes. If along one shore the cultivated fields of rice, barley, wheat and mustard reached nearly to the water's edge, on the opposite shore the sand bank extended uninterrupted for what seemed like miles. Along one of these gleaming, desert shores, women were washing clothes. In lieu of soap, they beat the clothes mercilessly on rocks, singing and chattering all the while. When the washing was done, they would extend the long, radiant lengths of saris between them and walk back through the shimmering expanse to some unseen village while the great ribbons of material the colour of poppies, lavender and lapis fluttered and dried in the hot breeze.

By late afternoon the course of the Ganges flowed in great sweeping bends. Cliffs pocked with caves rose up along the shore, and I could see a *sadhu* or two sitting in the thresholds and motionlessly contemplating the river. I tried to imagine the reaction from the clergy of the organized, institutional religions of the West to such an existence of radical, boundless freedom. It was inconceivable. If a Christian hermit were to try to subsist along the Thames, the Rhine, or the Mississippi, I'm certain that he would be labelled antisocial, a dangerous 'fringe' element, a parasite, and summarily run out of town.

Frankly, I found the freedom of worship which exists within the Hindu fold appealing. Hinduism is full of canonical doctrines which may not be dismissed without jeopardizing the faith. But while criticism is scarcely tolerated, interpretation is not only allowed, but encouraged. When a *sadhu* or a monk wanders the land offering sermons in the most remote village or in a city temple, he is bound by the sacred texts, but he is also the interpreter of the Writ. Just about the only commandment which is not open to interpretation is the central and unequivocal precept that no harm should come to human or animal life.

We had been on the river for three days when we came upon Bindhachal, a village perched high atop the cliffs on the right bank. The village didn't appear on my map, but it was obviously well known to Bola and Amer, both of whom became highly animated when the steep stone steps of the ghat came into view. Ordinarily, we struck up some sort of consensus as to where to stop along the journey, but in this instance, they steered straight for the shore and pulled at the oars with noticeable fervour.

'Devi! Durga!' said Amer, referring to the most sanguinary aspect of Shiva's consort Parvati who is often depicted wearing a necklace of sculls and wielding a sword. Bola clasped his hands together and bowed, saying *'puja'*.

They wanted to pay homage to the goddess. The point of *puja* is to receive *darsan*, literally 'vision' or 'sight' of a deity or a charismatic figure or object. The act is considered meritorious and an integral part of *dharma*, the totality of duties and observances enjoined in the sacred texts. To receive *darsan* is roughly equivalent to receiving a Christian blessing.

We landed near the ghat. Boys were swimming along the bank; women were thrashing clothes on the rocks; and a barber was shaving a devotee's head as clean as a golden orb. Bola and Amer went to the temple first while I stayed with the boat. What appeared to be half the population of the village came to stare at the sahib. They didn't attempt to communicate, or to sell me anything; they just stared guilelessly. After what seemed an eternity, Bola and Amer returned and relieved me of this silent torture. Their foreheads were daubed with vermilion tilak marks, and they were sporting garlands of marigolds. They looked surprisingly elated for having just visited the Goddess of Destruction.

I climbed the ghat and made my way up a narrow lane where toddlers were defecating in the open sewers, and skeletal dogs were fighting over minuscule scraps of food. A cow came down the lane and nearly tossed me into the reeking gutter. The street was lined with stalls selling red tilak powders, fruit, flowers and cloth. I bought a garland to offer to the goddess. As I drew closer to the temple, I could hear a clamour of drums, bells and chanting.

There was a considerable queue to catch a glimpse of Devi. I deposited my shoes on the steps of the temple, and after shuffling along with the frenzied crowd, I found myself treading through a coagulum of mud, water, flower petals, and other diluvian matter in a narrow chamber where Devi reigned behind a gilded cage. She had a black, doll-like head with sinister, silver eyes, her hair consisted of garlands of *java* flowers (China Rose), and her neck was brimming with marigolds. She was treading upon a rat and brandishing a sword. I don't scare easily, but Devi gave me the creeps. I tossed her the garland and fled. On the way out, a *panda* gave me a tilak mark. I wasn't sure whether I had been blessed or cursed.

At dusk, we sighted Mirzapur, the only town of any consequence that we had seen since setting off from Allahabad, but Bola and Amer didn't want to stop. They were boatmen and suspicious, if not downright fearful, of villages, towns, and civilization in general. I had no reason to insist that we stop; I too preferred the uninhabited banks, and so we drifted by and moored for the night on the opposite shore. The sun, as red as a tilak mark, sank behind Mirzapur and cast the immense sky with a

stratum of rather too-fierce colours. The waxing moon rose, quite
nearly full, and turned the surface of the Ganges into a swath of
luminous silver. Ducks flew overhead.

In the night, Bola woke me from the grips of a nightmare. I
was being pursued by the silver-eyed Devi and her rat. I ran
through the alleys of Bindhachal and when I reached the ghat, I
dived off the steps into a river of floating, chanting corpses.

We could have made it to Varanasi the following day, but I
was in no rush to get to terra firma. I told Bola that I wanted one
more day and night on the river, and that I wished to visit
Chunar, the site of a Moghul fort and quarries which have been
providing exquisite sandstone to palaces and temples for millennia. He didn't seem to be in much of a rush either. What's more,
Amer had become ill. I took his place at the right oar and he
stretched out to sleep.

The Ganges was remarkable for its lack of river traffic. But for
an occasional ferry, and the odd fishing boat, we hardly saw
other vessels. Soon after we set out in the morning, however,
we were passed by a boat that had all the grotesque qualities of a
hallucination. The bow was fitted with the head of an elephant,
an allusion to Lord Ganesh, the god of wisdom and remover of
obstacles; the stern swept up in the form of a fishtail. On the
upper deck rose a temple of gaudy columns, towers and domes
painted in a riotous palette. The rails were covered with tinsel.
A *sadhu* stood squarely on the bridge. Plying alongside was a
police boat weighed down to its gunwales with uniformed
bodyguards.

Bola called him *Ganga Baba*. Evidently he resided in Calcutta,
but often took to the river when his spirit moved him. It looked
like a wonderful way to travel. Bola and Amer clasped their
hands together and bowed as he passed, but *Ganga Baba* didn't

acknowledge the gesture; he stared ahead fixed and straight like a good captain.

At midday, we drifted into Chunar. The fort crowned a colossal promontory of sandstone that thrust into the river like the bow of a great transatlantic ship. There were boys playing cricket on the sandbank; and a flotilla of boats was just pushing off in a funeral procession. A *sadhu* had died, and they were rowing out to cast his unburned body into the current at midstream. I was sure we would meet him again later.

Amer slept; Bola went off to buy firewood; and I climbed up to the fort.

It was a dreary place, as might be expected of a citadel that had been alternately defended, sieged, occupied and regained by a steady stream of Moghuls, Pathans, Afghans and British since the early sixteenth century. In 1772, it fell into the hands of the East India Company, and later served as a refuge for British military invalids, a state prison, and finally a reformatory for boys. Now, it was abandoned.

Architecturally, it was of little interest, all undressed Cyclopean blocks of sandstone, barrack-like structure, and martial ramps, battlements, wards and courtyards. It did, however, afford expansive views over the Ganges and the surrounding countryside. It was nice to be on high for a change. When the sun grew unbearable, I stretched out in a shaded arcade, read Vedic hymns, and had a brief siesta.

When I returned to the boat, Amer had improved, and Bola was railing at mischievous urchins who were trying to climb aboard the boat. We pushed off in search of a safe and quiet place to pass the last night. Varanasi lay only fourteen miles downstream.

Despite a wood fire, a marginally less torrid dinner which Bola cooked in my honour, and a star-filled sky, it was a sad night. I didn't want to leave these boatmen. To me, they were remarkable for their simplicity, their knowledge of the river, and their quiet, unaffected devotion. Had I the time, I would have asked them to carry on to Calcutta.

Older than history, older than tradition, older even than legend, and looks twice as old as all of them put together. *Mark Twain on Varanasi*

In the harsh, unforgiving midday light there wasn't the slightest shadow to soften the vision of Varanasi. Along the left bank of the river, which stretched in a wide, flawless crescent, lay a tangled accumulation of ghats and palaces, temples and shrines, ashrams and pavilions, monasteries and *dharamshalas*, all of which appeared to be straining to step just one stride closer to the sacred shore, and in the case of the slightest misstep, to be likely to send the whole hallowed mass crashing into the river. Across the water came a steady, untiring roar, the combined effect of the pious praying, monks chanting, widows wailing, merchants hawking, children shrieking, and pilgrims by the thousands crying out in ecstasy as they spilled down the steps of the ghats and plunged into *Ganga Ma*. Only the meditators were silent, and the tourists. The latter stood on the ghats staring in disbelief, some enthralled, others aghast, their visions of the splendid mysteries of India rapidly disappearing in the face of the nightmarish reality. And then there was the smell, like nothing I had ever smelled before, but at the same time instantly identifiable; it was the stench of humanity, whole and unadulterated, lacking in nothing and enveloping everything. It was the smell of the living, and of the dead whose bodies burned and smouldered atop funeral pyres and sent flames spitting and smoke rising in acrid clouds of grey. I was at once enthralled and slightly sickened.

We landed at the Dashashwamedha Ghat, the 'ghat of the

ten-horse sacrifices', and we were immediately surrounded by the throng. This was not the atmosphere in which I had wanted to bid farewell to Bola and Amer, but there was little I could do to change it. I had given them their payment the night before, along with a whole host of items, from woollen gloves to a kerosene lamp, for which I no longer had a need. I clasped my hands before me and bowed low to them both. They did likewise, but Bola then stooped to touch my feet. I felt embarrassed and self-conscious at this show of respect, most of all because it was undeserved. It was I who should have touched their feet.

I ascended the ghat without looking back and disappeared into the multitude.

The name Varanasi is a contraction of 'Varuna' and 'Assi', the two streams which flow into the Ganges and mark the northern and southern boundaries of the ancient city. Benares or Banaras is nothing but a mispronounced version of Varanasi. Kashi, the 'city of light', is an old, pious moniker, and refers specifically to the holy terrain delineated by a near-circular road, more imagined than real, and absent from any map, known as the Panchakroshi. To die within this precinct, or in the Ganges itself, leads to an instant release from rebirth. Shiva himself is said to utter the *taraka-mantra*, the 'prayer of the crossing' that brings on *mukti*, into the dying person's ear.

Which is why, at all hours and at all times of the year, Varanasi is teeming, but never so much as on the nights when the moon is full.

And it was.

> I invoke the splendorous full moon night . . .
> may she listen to our prayers and accept them;
> may she blend our thoughts and actions into the universal melody.
>   *Rig Veda 2.33.4*

When the sun set, I stepped out of my guest house and into the crush. There was no question of which way to go; the sea of pilgrims was flowing towards the river and I let myself get swept up by the current. They had come from every corner of the subcontinent. There were Keralans, Bengalis and Punjabis, whole clans from Gujarat, masses from impoverished Bihar, desert people from Rajasthan, Tamils, Kashmiris and Goans. They marched and danced behind troupes playing reedy-pitched flutes and beating furiously on drums. Men were wielding snakes, torches, banners, and images of Shiva, Ganga and Vishnu. Pilgrims halted at temples and shrines along the route, offering *puja* and smearing lingams with vermilion powders in a clear allusion to ancient blood sacrifices. It was as frenzied a spectacle as I had ever witnessed, and there came a moment, as we drew near to the top of the Dashashwamedha Ghat, when I thought I was going to be swallowed up and trampled by the mob.

The Ganges was aflame with floating torches. At the water's edge rose a forest of tall, bamboo poles topped with lanterns. Boats were decked with candles; so too were the ghats, and palace windows, temple towers, and every other available recess and threshold. On a flower-decked stage at the foot of the ghat, a priest sat cross-legged, reciting passages from the Vedas. Flanking the stage were a series of smaller, elevated stages where male and female dancers clad in golden robes and saris enacted a pantomime. The moon hung over the Ganges like a perfectly placed golden sphere in a *mise en scène*. When the recitation drew to a close, the sky was illuminated with fireworks, and the crowd cheered wildly and pushed its way to the river's edge to raise the sacred waters in cupped hands and invoke the gods.

What a very evocative way, I thought, to pray.

I wandered through alleys and lanes so narrow there was scarcely room enough for two or three to walk abreast. There were no street lights, and everyone I passed took on a kind of phantasmagorical appearance. Shops were still doing business and I was invited to step in and peruse fine silks and silver, carved ivory, coloured glass, and artless clay figurines. Sassy young men emerged from the shadows and in poisonous whispers offered *charas* (hashish), opium and heroin. The city of light was also the city of death.

I became lost. Every labyrinthine lane led to another, equally constricted and strange. If I could only find the river, I thought, but every step seemed to take me deeper and deeper into the morass. I felt that mild form of panic that comes from the realization that here I could be swallowed up and disappear without the slightest trace, and no one would ever find me or my remains, and if anyone tried, they would stand before some thoroughly indifferent Indian official or policeman who would ask, 'But what was he doing in the back alleys of Varanasi in the middle of the night?' And they wouldn't know.

Finally, a kindly *sadhu*, his trident striking the ancient stones, led me through the maze and out to a busy road where I was able to hail a rickshaw. May Shiva bless the *sadhus*.

There is hardly a deity in the crowded Hindu pantheon who does not have a temple or a shrine in Varanasi, which accounts for the traditional claim that there are 108 or 1,008 temples in the city; and while neither of these figures is accurate, I would bet that the second is nearer the truth.

I spent the day touring temples. Many of these sanctuaries were located in the Vishwanatha Khanda, the oldest district of the city, and the very same neighbourhood where I had so thoroughly lost my bearings the night before. In the light of day, the place was still strange, but considerably less threatening.

I looked into the Annapurna Bhavani Temple, where the goddess, Kashi's Queen, took the benevolent form of the Mother of the Three Worlds. In her hand she held a cooking spoon. At the

Nepalese Temple, I found the atmosphere rather gloomy until I took a closer look at the wood carvings and lingered (perhaps too long) at the sight of deities performing imaginative erotic acts in the most improbable and acrobatic positions. I came face to face with the god known as the 'Black Terror' and considered the police chief of Kashi at the Kala Bhairava Temple. I gazed at the Wide-Eyed Goddess, the Love-Eyed Goddess and the Fish-Eyed Goddess. I observed statues of *ganas*, protectors of Kashi's sacred precinct, who bore the unflattering titles of Bell Ears, Cow Ears and Goat Face. At the Durga Temple, a place of rare calm sequestered behind vine-covered walls in the southern part of the city, monkeys were swinging from the *shikhara*, stalking the porticoes, and nearly set upon me when I tried to take an innocuous photograph of a water tank. At the Vishwanatha Temple, the most hallowed sanctuary in Varanasi, dedicated to Shiva as 'Lord of the Universe', however, I was forbidden entry. And just so I got the message, a disagreeable policeman who stood guard at the door waved his lathi in my face unprovoked, and reprimanded me in a burst of incomprehensible Hindi. No matter, there were temples enough to behold.

Yet for all the artistry of Varanasi's temples, and all the genuine outpouring of devotion which I observed, my temple tour had left me unsatiated. I missed the river. I returned to my guest house, gathered my gear, checked out, and headed straight for the Dashashwamedha Ghat where I promptly rented a houseboat. The vessel was moored just off the ghat and bore a fresh coat of paint in a sort of psychedelic motif of fiery orange, poisonous green and electric blue. When I descended to the cabin, however, I began to have second thoughts. To begin with, the air was laced with the smell of yesterday's curry. There was garbage strewn everywhere. The mattress was so soiled that it bore a sheen, and a good deal of its stuffing was scattered across the floor. I thought I heard scurrying. A rat? Or maybe just the ripples of the Ganges, I wasn't sure. I spent the better part of the evening swabbing, but I didn't care. I was back on the river.

For the following week, I barely left the ghats. Here, along the river, more than at Varanasi's temples and shrines, was where the sacred rites unfolded, and where pilgrims bathed and carried out their oblations, libations, and incidental offerings at every hour of the day and night. This is where the yogis sat, the swamis meditated, the Brahman priests offered *puja*, and the families of the dead carried their deceased on flower-decked litters chanting, '*Ram Nam Sach Hai*' ('The Name of God is Truth').

Tourists often stood in shock, compelled by a sense of morbid curiosity, at the Manikarnika Ghat, Varanasi's principal cremation ground, where the Untouchable guardians kept the funeral pyres burning; where families chanted and wailed as the corpses were consumed by the flames; and where buzzards circled patiently overhead. I had visited burning ghats before, the first at Pashupatinath in the Kathmandu Valley, and I had no ghoulish desire to linger before the grim scene. Let the living burn their dead in peace, I thought as I passed by the horror-struck audience of foreigners who didn't understand the ritual and likely never would.

I was far more interested in the *kund*, a tank or pool above the cremation grounds at Manikarnika which is said to be fed by a subterranean river that flows directly from the Cow's Mouth above Gangotri. Lord Vishnu carved out this *kund* with his discus at the time of the creation when the only firm ground which existed in the whole universe was that of Kashi. Hard by the *kund* is a marble slab imprinted with Vishnu's footprints, worn smooth by the touch of countless pilgrims. And unlike the footprints at Hardwar, no greedy *panda* demanded a fee.

*

Wandering along the ghats one evening I stopped at the Mir Ghat, which, despite a number of important shrines including the Well of Dharma, is a stretch of the riverfront traditionally intended for Varanasi's Muslim population, which is considerable. But for a young student reading his Koran, no one was about. I wanted to strike up a conversation with this young man awash in an ocean of infidels.

'A very good book,' I offered.

'The greatest book of all,' he said.

'Perhaps there are some people hereabout who wouldn't quite agree.'

'They are heathens and idolaters. They worship many gods, but there is only One God.'

This was an old gripe, and, what's more, a time-worn misconception. The sacred texts of Hinduism are quite clear in stating the Oneness of the Godhead, although that God presents itself in a great variety of aspects. I had spoken with a Hindu scholar a few days earlier who had offered an instructive analogy: every man is an individual, yet at the same time, he is a son; he may be a father and a husband too, and a brother. He may also be a doctor, and the president of a civic organization, and a musician. Still, he is but one man.

I mentioned this analogy to the young Muslim.

'These are Hindu lies,' he said.

I could see that he was beginning to seethe, so I left him to his hard, unwavering dogma. I sat on the steps some distance away, opened my notebook and read a Vedic stanza which I had thought worth transcribing:

O Lord of creatures, Father of all beings,
you alone pervade all that has come to birth.
Grant us our heart's desire for which we pray.
May we become the lords of many treasures!

*

It wasn't easy staying on in Varanasi. It wasn't just the filth, or the stench, or even the multitudes who seemed never to leave one's side, and prevented one from ever enjoying a brief moment of intimacy. What affected me most was my condition as a non-Hindu. I could sit along the ghats for hours at a time observing the faithful performing their time-honoured rites; I could visit the temples and shrines and marvel at their antiquity; I could converse with holy men, and wade through the holy literature. But for me, the waters of the Ganges did not possess the power to purify my soul; at the temples there was no *darsan*; the sages were enlightening surely, but they could not convert me into a Hindu; and while the Vedic hymns were exquisite, to me they were mere poetry. I was an outsider, a passive observer, a *mleccha*, and I always would be.

I woke up one star-soaked morning before the light of dawn. From the deck of my houseboat, I watched the first wave of bathers descend the ghat and begin their ritual prayers and libations, offerings and ablutions. In the shadows of the Shitala Temple, I could make out a frail, hoary figure at the water's edge. I had seen him every day, lying on a tattered mat, begging alms and awaiting death. Now, he was up and entering the river. Across his shoulders a pole was strapped bearing a clay pot at each end. He waded deeper. The pots floated on the river's surface. He waded deeper still. The pole tipped and one pot filled with water, then the other. His shoulders disappeared. He gasped a final breath in mid-prayer and his head sunk from view beneath the surface of the Ganges. In no other place would I have watched idly while such a scene unfolded before my eyes, but here in Varanasi, in Kashi, in this supreme *tirtha* or 'crossing place', I was powerless to stop him. Who was I to deny him a long-awaited salvation? In the name of what God?

3 / In the Footsteps of the Buddha

The Way exists but not the traveller on it. *Ancient Buddhist dictum*

In the elongated, early-morning shadow of a tamarind tree on the road from Varanasi to Sarnath, I came upon an ascetic sitting in meditation on a sinister bed of thorns. His body, rail-thin and withered, was smeared with ash, the pallor of his skin accentuating the wounds and scars of a soul bent on mortification. He was a devotee of Lord Shiva.

For an instant, I thought he was dead, but as I approached, he opened a pair of sunken eyes and stared ahead blankly. I laid some coins and fruit at his feet, but I had no desire to linger. My head was reeling with Vedic verses and images from esoteric rites, and my spirit dashed by a prolonged proximity to the dead and dying. I turned and continued on, leaving the ascetic to his austerities and the Hindu world behind. Before me lay a Buddhist geography, ruinous, but still spiritually charged, in which I longed to find a measure of peace.

When I had walked up the road a short distance, I looked back to see a vulture perched knowingly on a branch above the ascetic, craning its neck at imminent carrion.

Unlike the myth-inspired sacred sites of Hinduism, the stations of Buddhist pilgrimage in India trace the footsteps and spiritual progress of an historical figure. It is the story of Siddhartha Gautama (563–483 BC), the son of an aristocratic Hindu chieftain (some say king), who abandoned his family and the rarefied life of the pleasure palace, and walked into the night in search of the Truth. His progress from renunciation to realization,

and from enlightenment to Nirvana, can actually be charted
on the map. Like the Christian pilgrim who wanders the hills
and valleys of Palestine, the Buddhist strikes out on the dusty
trails of the Gangetic plain to walk where He walked; to dwell
where He dwelt. The paths and the holy places to which they
lead, to Bodh Gaya where the Buddha reached enlightenment;
to the deer park at Sarnath where he preached his first sermon;
or to the remote village of Kushinagara, the lonely site of the
Buddha's death, have come to form a sacred geography. It is to
these and other sites, ancient and time-worn, but still resonant
with the Buddha's message, that the pilgrim goes forth on both a
spiritual and a physical journey, at times bowing his head in
reverence, at others attempting to overcome the profane
obstacles which relentlessly arise on the road.

Had either the Buddha or Christ chosen a secluded, stationary
life, there would be no footsteps to follow. As it was, they both
exalted the peripatetic condition, and they both showed us a
Path; that one leads to Nirvana, and the other to salvation and
eternal life, are two very different spiritual prospects, but in both
cases it is the pilgrim, the soul seeking enlightenment, who
must set off on the journey. As the Buddha lay on his deathbed,
he offered his followers a simple, if telling, imperative: 'Walk on!'

They were waiting for me at a bend in the road, two diminutive
figures clad in the stiff, yellow robes of recently ordained *bhikkus*
or monks. Their finely shaven heads shone like gilded domes
under the sun. They had travelled from Thailand in search of the
Buddha, and a mere three miles outside Varanasi, halfway to
Sarnath, they were aghast at what they saw. If, according to
Buddhist scripture, the sight of an old man, a sick man, a corpse
and a mendicant ascetic had spurred Siddhartha to contemplate
the root of human suffering, well, I was told, they had seen
scores of all four. They wanted nothing so much as to return to

the security and unwavering routine of their monastery.

'In Sarnath, we will find the Buddha's spirit,' I said by way of encouragement, but they looked unconvinced and shuffled their sandalled feet in the dust.

'Buddha spirit also in the monastery,' one said.

'Ah, but the Buddha was never in your monastery and he was in Sarnath.'

This logic seemed to strike an emotional chord. An hour later, I walked into Sarnath flanked, rather ceremoniously, by *bhikkus*.

A vast excavated precinct revealed crumbling *stupas*, or reliquary mounds, the foundations of numerous ancient monasteries, and the odd remains of walls, pillars, promenades, pools and courtyards spread out over a landscape of immaculate, emerald- green lawns. There were Hindu families picnicking amidst the ruins; yellow, saffron and maroon-robed *bhikkus* and female *bhikkunis* circumambulating the *stupas*; and day-trippers out from Varanasi snapping photos of the tame deer.

I sat beneath a banyan tree and tried to envision the scene as it might have been at Sarnath over two thousand years ago, when the teachings of the Buddha were still new and radical, the monasteries were thriving with eager followers, and the throne of the Mauryan Empire was occupied by King Ashoka (273–232 BC), a former warrior whose conversion to the *dharma*, or law of Buddhism, ushered in a golden age.

Yellow-robed monks and nuns would have been studying, meditating, walking and discussing the Great Teacher's message. There would have been sculptors carving friezes and statues to adorn the *stupas*, and architects drawing up plans for yet another monastery. Pilgrims, patrons, merchants and wanderers would have been entering the gates to listen to the word, pay homage to the Buddha, or test the *dharma*; missionaries would have been

setting off bound for China, Syria, Greece, Egypt and Sri Lanka.
Everyone would most certainly have read, or been made to
understand, the fourteen edicts carved into the pillar erected by
King Ashoka:

Edict 1 forbade the slaughter of animals for sacrifice.

Edict 2 detailed the cultivation of herbs and fruits for
medicinal purposes, and the building of roads and wells.

Edict 3 instructed *Mahamatras* or 'Officers of Righteousness' to
spread the *dharma*.

Edict 4 elaborated on Edict 3.

Edict 5 urged subjects to help the families of prisoners and
criminals.

Edict 6 stated that Ashoka was available for counsel to any of
his subjects.

Edict 7 called for self-control and purity of thought.

Edict 8 described Ashoka's pilgrimages.

Edict 9 denounced superstitious rites.

Edict 10 denounced fame and glory.

Edict 11 expounded on the beneficial effects of *dharma*.

Edict 12 instructed *Mahamatras* to tolerate and encourage the
principles of all religions.

Edict 13 apologized for the razing and slaughter of Kalinga.

Edict 14 summarized the previous thirteen.

Ashoka signed himself as Piyadasi, 'the Humane', and
rightfully so.

It was at Sarnath that Buddhism was born, and after Bodh
Gaya, where Gautama reached enlightenment, it is Buddhism's
most hallowed ground. This was the place where the Buddha
chose to preach his first sermon, 'Setting in Motion the Wheel of
Dharma', to the five ascetics with whom he had fasted, meditated

and suffered austerities for six years before abandoning the mendicants and reaching enlightenment at Bodh Gaya.

What the Buddha preached at Sarnath became the bedrock of Buddhism: the Middle Way, the Four Noble Truths, and the Eightfold Path.

> Those foolish people who torment themselves, as well as those who have become attached to the domains of the senses, both of these should be viewed as faulty in their method, because they are not on the way to deathlessness. These so-called austerities but confuse the mind which is overpowered by the body's exhaustion. In the resulting stupor one can no longer understand the ordinary things of life, how much less the way to the Truth which lies beyond the senses. The minds of those, on the other hand, who are attached to the worthless sense-objects, are overwhelmed by passion and darkening delusion. They lose even the ability to understand the doctrinal treatises, still less can they succeed with the method which by suppressing the passions leads to dispassion. So I have given up both these extremes, and have found another path, a middle way. It leads to the appeasing of all ill, and yet it is free from happiness and joy. *Buddhacarita* or 'The Acts of the Buddha'

To follow the Middle Way, one must first grasp the Four Noble Truths: the existence of suffering, the root of suffering, the cessation of suffering, and the path which leads to the cessation of suffering.

In turn, the Way which leads to the cessation of suffering is an Eightfold Path: Right View, Right Thought, Right Speech, Right Action, Right Livelihood, Right Effort, Right Mindfulness, and Right Concentration.

It was a simple, if radical, message. Simple because liberation could be had, not from an accumulation of sacrifices, or the fortunes of birth, but through the cessation of desire and separate selfhood. Radical because it promoted morality without metaphysics. Compared with the elaborate rituals, the sacrifices, the constraints and the overcrowded pantheon of Brahmanism, Buddhism was a revelation.

> Do not what is evil. Do what is good. Keep your mind pure. This is the teaching of Buddha. *Dhammapada 183*

I scoured the ruins. There wasn't a hint of a breeze and the heat which rose from the baking Ashokan bricks was suffocating. There was, alas, precious little to see. Sarnath is less an evocative archaeological site than a heap of relentlessly plundered ruins. Were it not for the power of the message delivered here twenty-five centuries ago, the place would be hopelessly tragic.

I wandered over to the Dharmekha Stupa, which commemorates the spot where the Buddha preached his first sermon, and circumambulated in the company of saffron-robed *bhikkus* from Burma and lay Buddhists from Sri Lanka, Tibet, Japan and China. The Tibetans turned their prayer wheels and beat diminutive drums, others chanted. I focused on the fifth-century Guptan reliefs on the exterior of the *stupa*. The only Indians I saw were a family sleeping off their lunch under a tree, and a group of Untouchable women squatting on a lawn nearby, patiently cutting the grass by hand.

I had often heard the disappearance of Buddhism in the land of its birth characterized as an enigma. To me, it was nothing of the sort. Between the merciless sword of first Hunnish and later a series of Muslim invaders, and the animosity of Brahman priests and theologians, Buddhism scarcely had a chance.

The successive waves of Muslim armies which swept over Northern India beginning in the eighth century treated the pacific Buddhists just like any other infidels: monks and nuns were murdered, monasteries sacked, and libraries burned. When the Muslim chieftain Bakhtiar Khalji entered Nalanda, the great seat of Buddhist learning, in 1199, he put over five thousand monks and nuns to the sword. There was no resistance; there couldn't have been – on the question of non-violence, the Great Teacher had been unequivocal:

> If men speak evil of you, this must you think: 'Our heart shall not waver; and we will abide in compassion, in lovingkindness, without resentment. We will think of the man who speaks ill of us with thoughts of love, and in our thoughts of love shall we dwell. And from that abode of love we will fill the whole world with far-reaching, wide-spreading, and boundless love.'
>
> Moreover, if robbers should attack you and cut you in pieces with a two-handed saw, limb by limb, and one of you should feel hate, such a one is not a follower of my gospel. *Majjhima Nikaya*

The Buddhists died as submissively as Christians in the Roman circus who went to their death empowered by Jesus's injunction: 'Do good to them that hate you.'

To the Brahman hierarchy, the Buddhist message was as cataclysmic as the tenets of Christianity would be for orthodox Judaism. Buddhism's rejection of the caste system and insistence on the existence of a Supreme Being threatened the Hindu tradition at its doctrinal core. For at least three or four hundred years after the Buddha's death, converts flocked to the Buddhist monasteries in droves, especially during the reign of Ashoka, when Buddhism enjoyed the status of a state religion.

The reaction of the Hindu pandits was nothing if not expedient; they absorbed the Buddha into their expansive pantheon as an avatar of Vishnu and a reviler of the Vedas.

By the twelfth century, Buddhism had been all but erased from India, a victim of Muslim fanaticism and the jealousies of the rival Brahman creed. For nearly a millennium there was silence, until British archaeologists started uncovering remains in the last century, and Buddhist pilgrims began to turn up once again, from Japan, Sri Lanka, Thailand, China, Burma, Tibet and the West; from everywhere, indeed, but India.

There wasn't a bed to be had in Sarnath, not in the *dharamshala* or the Government Tourist Bungalow, or any of the modern temples maintained by the Buddhist nations of Asia. I settled on a patch of grass among the Tibetan refugees, who had set up a makeshift camp in the shadows of their temple. As night fell, I huddled in a tea stall full of ruby-robed monks and novices and their dishevelled countrymen, and read from the *Dhammapada*, perhaps the most celebrated collection of aphorisms attributed to the Buddha.

> If month after month with a thousand offerings for a hundred years one should sacrifice; and another only for a moment paid reverence to a self-conquering man, this moment would have greater value than a hundred years of offerings.
>
> If a man for a hundred years should worship the sacred fire in the forest; and if another only for a moment paid reverence to a self-conquering man, this reverence alone would be greater than a hundred years of worship.
>
> Whatever a man for a year may offer in worship or in gifts to earn merit is not worth a fraction of the merit earned by one's reverence to a righteous man.

Over four days, I walked and rode in an occasional bullock cart through a landscape of rice paddies, wheat fields, and miserable red-clay villages, before arriving at dusk in Bodh Gaya, the *axis mundi* of the Buddhist world.

At the Burmese *vihara*, or monastery, a young gatekeeper in wrap-around sunglasses and a black mock-leather jacket led me through a courtyard, where mongrel dogs eyed me from the shade and monks sat bent over sacred books, to a spartan cell. In front of the cell next door, a rather bedraggled-looking German couple, no longer young, were speaking in a querulous tone. When they saw me, they edged over to share their burden. It seemed a travelling companion of theirs had been missing for three days.

'He goes to Mahakala Caves for the day,' said the woman, 'but doesn't come back.'

The gatekeeper looked unfazed.

'Have you gone to the police?' I asked.

'*Na ja, polizei,*' said the man, 'want dollars!'

'Have you gone off looking for him?'

'We are in meditation course, we cannot leave now,' she said. 'We are very close.'

I wasn't quite sure to what they were so close, but it was clear that their meditation was more important than their friend.

The gatekeeper shuffled off without a word.

'Indians,' said the woman in disgust as she watched him depart, 'they are filthy people.'

'Actually, he's Burmese,' I corrected her. I didn't add that he looked a good deal cleaner than either of them.

They retreated into their cell to pursue their enlightenment.

I walked out of the monastery in the half-light, bound for the Mahabodhi Temple. It was a half-mile stroll to the temple complex. The unpaved road was lined with tented tea shops with names like 'Gautama Café' and 'The Dharma Lounge'. There were stalls selling beads, flowers, incense and candles. The misnamed 'Shiva Travel' specialized in bus tours of the Buddhist circuit. Rickshaw drivers rang their bells, pleading for a fare. Through the trees I could make out the black current of the Phalgu river.

When I reached the temple gate, I was set upon by a legion of urchins and beggars with unspeakable infirmities. A man with a leprous, half-eaten face tugged at my sleeve. I didn't stop. As soon as I crossed the threshold, there was calm.

The entire sunken temple precinct was aflame with the light from thousands of candles and tallow lamps, the 'lake of fire' which E M Forster described on his visit here. The pyramidal, nine-storeyed temple spire soared from a broad plinth to a height of 180 feet; its surface was carved with lotus flowers, niches, string courses, mouldings, and a multitude of miniature Buddhas. At the summit rose a gold finial. Buddhist lore attributes the temple to Ashoka, but archaeologists reckon the most ancient parts of the edifice date from the Kushana period (50 BC – AD 200). Its architect is unknown.

Spreading out around the temple, flickering in the light, was a studied landscape of flagstoned alleys and paths which led to *stupas* and shrines where pilgrims walked, prostrated themselves, and sat in meditation. The whole numinous scene was accompanied by the low murmur of collective chanting.

I followed a group of white-robed pilgrims into the sanctum sanctorum of the temple and bowed, but didn't prostrate myself, before the golden image of the Buddha, depicted with his hand touching the ground, hailing Mother Earth to witness his awakening. The statue was flanked by vases full of peacock feathers, and surmounted by a baldachin of rather cheesy gauze. From behind me someone whispered in my ear, 'May the Buddha bless you.'

At the rear of the temple, in a sanctuary enclosed by a finely carved sandstone railing, stood a pipal or fig tree of the species *Ficus religiosa*, a descendant of the Bodhi or 'Enlightenment' tree under which Gautama sat and resolved not to stir until he had attained enlightenment. In that night he grasped the insight which is at the heart of true Buddhist liberation: that impermanence and emptiness of self are precisely the conditions on which life depends. Gautama's liberation, his ascent to Buddhahood and his brush with Nirvana inspired the two renowned, often-quoted verses from the *Dhammapada*:

> I have gone round in vain the cycles of many lives ever striving to find the builder of the house of life and death. How great is the sorrow of life that must die!
>
> But now I have seen thee, housebuilder: never more shalt thou build this house. The rafters of sin are broken, the ridgepole of ignorance is destroyed. The fever of craving is past: for my mortal mind is gone to the joy of the immortal Nirvana.

I sat beneath the Bodhi tree amidst a bevy of Buddhists from Asia. They were all deep in meditation, except one elderly man chanting '*Om Mani Padme Hum*' ('Hail to the Jewel in the Lotus'). The trunk of the Bodhi tree was wrapped in gold fabric, and multi-coloured prayer flags were draped from its branches. The leaves were the shape of hearts. Propped against one of the roots was a sign which read: PLEASE DO NOT PLUCK LEAVES FROM THE SACRED BO TREE. DO NOT HAVE SOIL FROM THE BO TREE. KINDLY SAVE THE SACRED BO TREE. Evidently, over-zealous pilgrims had been treating the tree to a slow death.

I crossed my legs and tried to meditate, but after a quarter of an hour or so, I gave up, not because of any external distractions – on the contrary, the scene was a picture of tranquillity – but rather for some very persistent inner rumblings. To arrive at Buddhism's most hallowed ground, plant myself beneath the Bodhi tree, and attempt to meditate without rigorous preparation seemed to me, at best, fallacious, at worst, positively fraudulent. I had, it's true, steeped myself in the sacred texts, and I found the message contained in the *Buddhacarita*, the *Dhammapada*, the sutras, and the *Lotus of the Good Law*, among other indispensable works, to be both ethically convincing and aesthetically appealing. It was not, however, enough.

Or maybe it was.

> Better than a hundred years lived in vice, without contemplation, is one single day of life lived in virtue and in deep contemplation.

And so I sat in quiet contemplation. Better to be overcome with humility, I thought, than to be greedy for enlightenment.

When a caretaker came to lock up the enclosure for the night, I was alone; the sky was luminous with stars and a half-moon; and all but a few isolated candles had been consumed. In front of the temple gates, the beggars lay wrapped in their shawls, sleeping in momentary peace. I emptied my pockets at their feet.

At first light I was back. It was too early for the tourists, but the temple compound was already teeming with *bhikkus*, lamas and pilgrims. I wandered among the shrines which commemorate the sites where the Buddha meditated following his enlightenment. There was the Animesa Locana, 'The Place of the Unwinking Gaze', where the Buddha spent a full week staring at the Bodhi tree without so much as a blink; the Cankamana, a cloister walk where lotus flowers carved into a raised platform indicate the spots where the Lord's feet trod; and the Ajapala Nigrodha, the banyan tree where the Buddha replied to a Brahman that only by one's deeds does one become a Brahman, not by birth. I liked this last shrine the most; its significance was not unlike the Christian message being spread to the Gentiles. Buddhism, like Christianity, arose as a light for all humankind, not merely for the twice-born, or those of a chosen people.

As I sat taking notes in the cool shadow of a *stupa*, a tousled *bhikku* planted himself over my shoulder.

'You are Englishman?'

'No.'

'Then you are Japanese,' he said, offering a rather odd alternative.

'Also not, guess again.' But he seemed to have exhausted his possibilities and just stared at me plaintively.

'I'm American.'

'Where is America?'

'Very far away.'

'East or West?'

'It's just about equidistant.'

'You are a Buddhist?'

'No, just an admirer of the Buddha.'

'What God do you have?'

'A Christian God, I think.'

'You are not sure?'

'Sometimes not.'

'I am a Buddhist. The Lord Buddha is my God.'

'I didn't think that Buddhists conceived of the Buddha as a God.'

'Buddha is my God!' he shouted in a very unBuddhalike manner.

'I'm sure he is.'

'You will give me money,' he said, extending a filthy hand.

'No.'

'Then you will give me your watch.'

'I'm afraid not.'

'Your camera.'

This was becoming tiresome. I changed the subject. 'Where are you from?'

'I am from here, from Bodh Gaya.'

'Ah, an Indian Buddhist.'

'The Buddha was Indian! These people you see here, they are not Indians. This is our temple!'

Here, I thought, was all the ethnocentric prejudice of Hinduism draped in a saffron robe. When a group of Japanese pilgrims passed, he set on them with equal resolve. 'You are English?' The Japanese took him for what he was, namely, deranged, and quickened their pace. I went off to practise some more tentative meditation beneath the Bodhi tree, the one place in Bodh Gaya where one is sure to be left in peace.

The revivification of Bodh Gaya and the restoration of its temple and shrines were made possible largely by the efforts of two men, Angarika Dharmapala and Sir Edwin Arnold; the former, a Sri Lankan Buddhist and founder of the Maha Bodhi Society; the latter, a Christian Englishman, poet, journalist and adventurer. They were an unlikely pair devoted to a common cause.

On pilgrimage to Bodh Gaya in 1891, Dharmapala was shocked to find the temple in the hands of a Saivite priest, the statue of the Buddha transformed into a Hindu icon, and the way barred to Buddhist worship.

Reverently I visited the brick temple, built in the form of a pyramid, and examined the carvings on the ancient railing. But I was filled with dismay at the neglect and desecration about me. The *mahant* – the head of the Hindu fakir establishment – had disfigured the beautiful images. At the end of a long pilgrimage, the devout Buddhist was confronted with monstrous figures of Hindu deities. It seemed an outrage that this holiest temple of the Buddhists should be under the management of a man whose ancestors had always been hostile to Buddhism.

I had intended to stay a few weeks and then return to Ceylon, so I had only a few *rupees* with me. But, when I saw the condition of the shrine, I began an agitation to restore it to Buddhist control. I communicated with the leading Buddhists of the world and urged them to rescue Bodhi Gaya from the Siva-worshipping Hindu fakirs. On May 31, 1891, I started the Maha Bodhi Society, to rescue the holy Buddhist places and to revive Buddhism in India, which for seven hundred years had forgotten its greatest teacher.

Today, the Maha Bodhi Society is the principal caretaker of the Buddhist holy places in India and a major charitable institution. At Bodh Gaya, the society maintains a primary school, a clinic, a library and a pilgrim shelter.

The fakirs, however, are still in residence. Hard by the entrance to the temple they maintain a shrine, and are fond of scandalizing the Buddhist pilgrims with Hindu rites and Vedic chants. On occasion, Buddhist and Hindu adepts have been known to come to blows.

If Angarika Dharmapala's appeal went out to his fellow Buddhist brethren, it was Sir Edwin Arnold who brought the Lord Buddha's message to the masses in the English-speaking West.

In 1879, Arnold published *The Light of Asia*, an epic poem which hailed the life and teachings of the Buddha. The work was an instant success both in England and America and won praise for its wealth of local colour (Arnold had spent several years as a schoolmaster at the Sanskrit College in Poona, and he knew the subcontinent well). The poem did, however, have its detractors. Oriental scholars criticized its simplification of Buddhist doctrine. Devout Christians took offence at Arnold's analogy between the Lord Buddha and the Lord Jesus Christ.

Nevertheless, through Arnold's flowery Victorian verse, masses of English-speaking readers got their first taste of the Great Teacher.

> Lo! the Dawn
> Sprang with Buddh's victory! Lo! In the East
> Flamed the first fires of beauteous day, poured forth
> Through fleeting folds of Night's black drapery . . .

Like Angarika Dharmapala, Arnold too went on a pilgrimage to Bodh Gaya, and while no Buddhist, his sensibilities were likewise offended. Upon returning to England, he published an article in the *Daily Telegraph* entitled 'East and West – A Splendid Opportunity' which revealed the lamentable state of Buddhism's most sacred sites. Suddenly, the restoration of Bodh Gaya became a *cause célèbre* and funds and pilgrims followed.

Had it not been for Dharmapala and Arnold, Bodh Gaya might well have remained ruined and forgotten, its glory obscured by Brahman usurpers.

They warned me not to travel alone, especially on foot. In this, the *bhikku*-in-charge at the Burmese *vihara*, the taciturn gatekeeper, the proprietor of the Gautama Café, and the venerable Maitipe Wimalasara Thera, high priest of the Maha Bodhi Society, were all in agreement; perhaps the last put it most plainly: 'They will kill you.' But he gave me his blessing anyway, as well as a copy of the *Visuddhi Magga*, 'The Path of Purification', an encyclopedic work on Theravada Buddhism that ran to 885 pages of excruciatingly fine print.

In fact, I was leaving Bodh Gaya reluctantly. While I had not experienced any flash of enlightenment beneath the Bodhi tree, or any monumental moments of insight, I was flush with the Buddhist message of compassion, mercy, love, devotion, serenity, meditation and introspection. I found, gratefully, no harping on sin. Man is not belittled in order to exalt the Buddha. Every individual, like the Buddha, has the potential for perfection. Nor was there any obstacle to joining the Buddhist fold, no status based on arbitrary bloodlines, no baptism, bar mitzvah, or secret initiation. It was enough to affirm the Three Refuges: I take Refuge in the Buddha; I take Refuge in the Dharma; I take Refuge in the Sangha.

When I walked out of Bodh Gaya, the German was still missing; a group of Taiwanese pilgrims, haggard and half-asleep, was filing off a bus; and the dawn light had transformed the surface of the Phalgu river into molten gold.

It *was* dangerous to walk alone. Bodh Gaya, Rajagriha, my next destination, and many of the places where the Buddha wandered are located in Bihar (from *vihara*, or monastery), India's poorest state, its most illiterate, and as lawless a place as the world knows. In the first six months of 1996, Bihar reported 2,625 murders, 1,243 kidnappings, and over 60,000 other violent crimes; that's an average of fourteen murders a day and one kidnapping every four hours.

The urgent, colourful prose of the *Times of India* painted the scene in Bihar thus:

> Gangsterism and the mafia raj in Bihar are going full throttle having acquired their full, turbo power. In West Champaran district, for instance, where kidnapping for ransom has become a cottage industry, blind hatred for the perceived enemy is the reigning ideology. This hatred is unfathomable and alive. Bhagad Yadav, Lalu Yadav, Ram Bhaju Yadev, Ram Singh, Allaudin Mian and Ram Basi Koeri are names which strike terror in the minds of young and old alike. In an atmosphere of lawlessness beyond any sense of proportion and shame some crimes committed by them veer into the surreal.

The article went on to describe (with equal flair) tales of caste wars, murder, rape and robbery, and ended on a decidedly grim note: 'Bihar has for decades symbolized the "end of order". That the State is slip-sliding into the abyss is no great news.'

The Buddha spirit, it seemed clear, had most definitely been erased from the land of his ministry.

The countryside between Bodh Gaya and Rajagriha stretched out in a succession of palmyra palm groves, rice paddies, and fields of wheat and sugarcane. Tiger grass grew along the sides of streams, and tamarind and crimson-blossomed sal trees provided a measure of shade. Everywhere there was dust. On the horizon, the Barabar Hills rose in the haze. No traffic came along the road all day except for an occasional horse-drawn *tonga* or a bullock cart; their drivers stared at me, speechless, as they passed. When I came upon a group of village girls shaping dung cakes and singing by the side of the road, they covered their faces with their hands and ran into a field shrieking. Communication with the locals, I could see, was going to be tricky.

As the sun was dropping behind the crest of the Barabar, I made camp in a palm grove. It took me nearly two hours to gather enough wood for a fire. I fixed curry, sunk into *The Path of Purification*, and listened to the whooping calls of a mina bird. Later, the night was full of wild dogs and jackals, and stars peeking through the fronds of the palms.

The following day, the road narrowed to a track and led through a series of mud-hut hamlets, where the men sat idly, the women worked tirelessly, and the children rolled in the dirt with the dogs and stray cattle. When I strolled through, all activity, such as it was, would come to a sudden halt. Then the mongrels would set on me, followed by the children, and finally the hollow-eyed elders. They would press around and gape.

In one of these cheery, nameless villages, I stopped for the night.

For all their initial suspicions, the villagers' mood changed abruptly when I asked, in halting Hindi punctuated by child-like gestures, to pass the night among them. At once, they became model hosts. The Sanskrit word for guest is *atithi*, 'one who comes unannounced', and he is treated as unto a god, which in Hindu tales is very often what he is. I was led to the shade of a banyan tree, a place of honour in rural India, accompanied by a wizened patriarch. The other men and boys squatted around according to their place in the village hierarchy. A file of women, barefoot and bangled, brought me water with which to wash, a bowl of buttermilk, and a melon.

When I indicated that I was bound for Rajagriha, the name only elicited a vague wagging of heads. Nor had they ever heard of the Buddha. I don't think there was one among them who could read. They were of low caste and didn't own the land they farmed. They possessed nothing.

I spent the afternoon treating a number of sundry illnesses: cuts, burns, colds and fevers; nothing that required anything more than an aspirin, vitamins, antiseptic cream or a clean band-age. Soon enough, however, an alarmingly long line had formed, and I went to great pains trying to tell them that I was, in fact, no doctor. It was useless; hope is eternal. An ancient man was led before me, his eyes milky white from river blindness. I shook my head in despair and pronounced the dispensary closed.

I had wanted to sleep under the banyan tree, but after dinner, I was shown to a hut that had been vacated for my benefit. To refuse this sign of hospitality would have been unthinkable. Like everything else in the village, the hut was built of mud brick and the thatched roof was covered in a tangle of squash vines. There was one door and no windows. Just outside the threshold stood the hearth. Inside, the earthen floor had been relentlessly pounded until its surface resembled polished Florentine marble. But for a charpoy on which to sleep, a blanket, some odd cooking utensils, and a modest shrine decorated with an image of Shiva torn from a magazine, there was nothing.

Before falling off to sleep, I read from the *Dhammapada* in the contrasting light of the Shiva lamp.

> If on the journey of life a man can find a wise and intelligent friend who is good and self-controlled, let him go with that traveller; and in joy and recollection let them overcome the dangers of the journey.
>   But if on the journey of life a man cannot find a wise and intelligent friend who is good and self-controlled, let him then travel alone, like a king who has left his country, or like a great elephant alone in the forest.

Looming above me when I opened my eyes in the morning was the figure of a grown man dressed in a woman's bathrobe printed with a motif of delicate white roses on an electric-blue background. I had, by chance, witnessed stranger things in India, but usually not quite so early in the morning. And then I saw that he had a gun, a steel-grey revolver with a grip wrapped in white medical tape. I was motioned to get up. There was another man standing in the threshold; he didn't have a gun, just a machete. I dressed, shaking. No one said a word.

Outside, three more men, one of whom was holding a very convincing sawn-off shotgun, stood surrounding the hut's owner, a shrivelled old man in a soiled *dhoti*. That he looked positively terror-struck made me even more nervous. One kidnapping every four hours, I thought; fourteen murders a day. Like a great elephant alone in the forest indeed. I recalled the voice of the high priest at Bodh Gaya, 'They will kill you.' In my mind's eye I saw my sons, fatherless. I broke into a cold sweat.

The man in the blue bathrobe began to question the villager. I couldn't follow a word of the exchange, but the gist, no doubt, was, who was I, where had I come from, and what was I doing there? The villager stuttered his replies, never looking up. When his interrogator didn't like a response, he waved his gun around furiously. Finally, the poor man fell to his knees and began to grovel. It looked very much as if he was asking for mercy. The other men laughed; and then they suddenly grew silent and looked at me. I resisted falling to my knees. For a long time they just stared. When I tried to help up the villager, I was pushed away. One of the men went into the hut and came out with my backpack and a smaller daypack full of my books. The leader, clearly the man in blue, gestured for me to open the bags with the assured air of a customs officer. I set out my possessions neatly in the dirt. They began to pick at will. Their selections, I thought, were telling. They took all my food, a pot, a flashlight, and some tongs. Shorts and trousers didn't interest them, although some lovely cotton material from Varanasi did. I imagined them fashioning some fine *dhotis*. Two of the men argued over some beads, and the leader snatched up all my tobacco. When I opened the pack with my books, they waved them away. At the sight of my stock of medicines, however, they were filled with quiet awe. Here, I hoped, was my chance.

I spread out the pills, creams, bandages, and rubbing alcohol on a clean white towel. I moved very slowly and methodically, like a priest preparing an altar for Mass. Over each item I mumbled something innocuous. I then motioned to the leader to sit by my side. He handed the revolver to one of his cohorts and squatted in front of me. Picking up a packet of aspirin as if it were some mysterious potion, I mimicked a splitting headache; with the vitamins, I first played fatigued and then inflated my chest and flexed my muscles. I held my stomach and doubled over to portray someone in need of an antibiotic. The dysentery sequence had them howling with laughter. But they were rapt. Only the day before I had been trying to convince the locals that I was not a doctor; now, I had to assume the role of the most thoroughly competent general practitioner that these men had ever set eyes on.

Gently, I took the leader's arm and played at taking his pulse. I had him roll his eyes, stick out his tongue, and expose his gums. I adopted a bedside manner at once informed and nurturing. I thought of Dr Schweitzer among the natives. I questioned my patient, again by way of pantomime, about his bowel movements, his sleeping habits, his diet. All thoroughly professional. I proceeded to prescribe two multi-vitamin tablets a day, one aspirin after breakfast, and a toothbrush to clean his foul mouth. I dressed a nasty wound on his shin. By the time his visit to the 'doctor' was through, the leader was smiling; he seemed genuinely grateful; it looked as if he felt better. And then, still smiling, he poked at my hip pouch, as if to say, what have you got there? I withdrew a substantial wad of *rupees*. He caressed the bills from my hand; he was radiant. Now, he gestured, he felt much better.

I was confined to the hut. The shotgun toter squatted in the doorway. And my daintily clad captor went off to celebrate his recuperated health with some fresh currency.

I lay on the bed and considered my fate. Thus far, I had managed to hold on to my books, my clothes and my life, and, in the process, had adopted a new profession. The future, however, looked bleak, although some scenarios were clearly worse than others. I could be led off to some barren tract and, say, have my head severed from my body with a swish of the machete; that was the dire, pathological option. I could also be held for ransom, the economic option, and spend several months in living hell, never quite sure that the money would, in fact, turn up. I did not see my mother, God bless her, selling the family silver to get me out of India. Finally, there was the blessed, brotherly option; I could be set free unscathed.

The Buddhist broods on the body's impermanence, but I prayed long and hard to save mine.

I found it impossible to read, much less to write. I paced the interior of the hut, a diminutive five strides and a heel, until I was bouncing off the walls. All the while, my keeper watched me impassively. I looked into his dark, slightly feminine eyes and tried to determine whether or not this was the face of my executioner. He seemed hardly to blink or breathe or register any expression. I took this as a bad sign. A natural born killer, I thought, he was probably dying to waste me.

Happily, the leader, this petty gangster of the mafia raj, as the *Times of India* might say, had a toothache. I was marched to the banyan tree to examine the patient. His mouth was flaming red with betel juice; still, I could see the rotten molar. He was, I was pleased to observe, in considerable discomfort. Nevertheless, ever the professional, I prescribed two aspirins and had him bite down on a third placed atop the bad tooth, a wonderful technique to ease the momentary pain, and a treatment guaranteed to eventually rot the tooth beyond redemption.

I was given a bowl of lentils and unleavened bread. My patient alternately winced and watched me eat. When I had finished, he took a stick and traced a sickle in the dirt. So, he was not merely a thief and a tyrant, but a comrade! He passed the stick to me and motioned for me to define myself. This was a hard enough task even when I had the luxury of words; reduced as I was to semiotics, I found myself rather at a loss. Finally, I flattened a broad area in the dust with my hand and sketched a trident, an eight-spoked wheel, a cross, a star of David, and a sickle moon; I then traced a generous circle to encompass them all. He studied my ecumenical doodling with an expressionless face. I had the uneasy sensation that my future might depend on this man's reading of ancient, sacred signs etched ephemerally in the dust of a godforsaken Indian village. After an insufferable silence, he at last rose, stood above my sacred circle, and erased each sign in turn with a calloused foot. He then delivered the *coup de grâce*, spitting a stream of betel juice into the dust at my feet.

As I was being escorted back to my prison-hut, I wondered if perhaps I should have included the hammer and sickle as well.

In the morning, villagers were peering in through the threshold and chattering excitedly. The blue-robed one and his merry
band were gone, just as quickly and quietly as they had come.

I felt like Daniel sprung from the lion's den. The locals,
however, were morose. They referred to my captors as *dacoits*,
roughly brigands or outlaws, and made me to understand that
they too had been robbed, not of *rupees* (they had none), but of
food stores. What's more, I gathered it was a regular event. They
were full of shame that I had been disgraced in their village.
They wanted me to stay, to make it up to me. I wanted only to
leave. I was free.

At my send-off under the banyan tree, the women sang and
swayed. I was presented with three mangos and some delicate
sweets wrapped in banana leaves. I bowed low, thanked them
profusely, and bolted.

The ancient track to Rajagriha climbed north into stony hills
thick with cactus, thorn shrubs, and wild indigo. The heat was
infernal. At the crest of the hill, I sat beneath a solitary pine and
feasted on the mangos. Before me stretched a landscape of
grey-green hills each crowned with a white Jain temple. Further
off, I could just make out Rajagriha, floating like an island in the
liquid heat.

As dusk was falling, I reached the ruins of walls, towers and
battlements that marked the boundaries of ancient Rajagriha;
together with the surrounding hills, they must have provided
a formidable defence. In the Buddha's day, the city was the
imperial capital of the Northern Indian kingdom of Magadha,
and Bimbisara, an enlightened monarch, provided patronage
to both the Buddha and his contemporary the Mahavira or
'Great Hero', the founder of Jainism.

It was King Bimbisara, the Buddha's first royal convert, who granted the *sangha*, or Buddhist Order, their first tract of land. The early Buddhists were, above all, wandering alms-seekers, perpetual pilgrims whose home was the road, the riverbank and the forest. Their only cause to stop moving was meteorological: the monsoons. Driven by the rains, the Lord Buddha and his followers made a seasonal retreat, the *vassa*, to the hills of Rajagriha, to a place known as the Bamboo Grove. The foundation of Buddhist monasticism can be traced to the moment in which the *sangha* ceased, if only momentarily, to wander.

To say that modern-day Rajagriha, also known as Rajgir, is a shadow of its former glory would be kind. In place of the former imperial capital I found a shabby market town overtaken by a plague of green, winged, nocturnal insects.

I sat in the dining room of the Green Hotel. The windows were closed to keep out the bugs and the air was stifling. The bugs got in anyway. I watched them swarm the lights outside in clouds as thick as locust.

'They come twice a year,' said the sweat-soaked proprietor. 'They stay for a week and then they are gone. It is a pity, so many are killed.'

'People?' I asked, astonished.

'No, no, the little creatures.'

When he served me dinner, he looked mournfully at the insects struggling in my curry. For his sake and mine, I picked the creatures gingerly from my plate before consuming my food with gusto. It had been days since I'd had a proper meal.

After dinner, I tied a scarf around my face and stumbled through the buzzing darkness to the Government Tourist Bungalow. I thought I deserved a bed.

The hotel was a two-storey cinder-block structure situated on a lonely plot about a mile outside of town. I walked past a night watchman hidden beneath a blanket to avert the insects.

Reception was empty, so too were the halls. At the rear was a riotous, weed-choked garden. I called out and finally roused the manager. He emerged from one of the rooms hoisting up his grey pyjamas. He was pale-skinned and creased. Before seeing to me, he went off and kicked the formless mass under the blanket who was presumably guarding the door. Although I was, by the look of it, the sole guest, the manager seemed a bit annoyed to see me. As I checked in, he tapped his gold rings incessantly on the counter. I had the feeling someone was waiting for him.

My room, the manager announced triumphantly, 'possessed' a view of the garden and an attached bath. It also had a smart assortment of broken furniture, a hopelessly stained, blood-red carpet, and a ceiling fan that whirled threateningly overhead. The walls were grey and decorated, for the time being, with a family of geckos.

I bathed, slipped between moderately clean sheets, and read in the glare of a bare bulb. From what I gathered, my recent mis-adventure on the pilgrimage trail was neither new nor especially beastly. In *A Record of the Buddhist Religion as Practised in India and the Malay Archipelago*, the seventh-century Chinese pilgrim I-Tsing describes a brush in Bihar with some of the blue-robed one's forebears:

> Late in the day, when the sun was about to set, some mountain brigands made their appearance; drawing a bow and shouting aloud, they came and glared at me, and one after another insulted me. First they stripped me of my upper robe, and then took off my under garment. All the straps and girdles that were with me they snatched away also. I thought at that time, indeed, that my last farewell to this world was at hand, and that I should not fulfil my wish of a pilgrimage to the holy places. Moreover, if my limbs were thus pierced by the points of their lances, I could never succeed in carrying out the original enterprise so long meditated. Besides,

there was a rumour in the country of the West [India] that, when they took a white man, they killed him to offer a sacrifice to heaven [Devas]. When I thought of this tale, my dismay grew twice as much. Thereupon I entered into a muddy hole, and besmeared all my body with mud. I covered myself with leaves, and supporting myself on a stick, I advanced slowly.

I went to sleep feeling fortunate to have come away with my clothes, and to have been spared the experience of besmearing my body with mud.

In the morning, I made straight for the Bamboo Grove, where I found a delightful park with tamarind and sal trees, bottle palms and kamala, banyan, eucalyptus, silver oaks, and not a single stalk of bamboo.

I sat in a pavilion overlooking a reflecting pool and tried to conjure up a monastery constructed not of hewn stone or baked brick, but of delicate bamboo. I envisioned the Buddha's hut, a simple dwelling with a floor of pounded earth, a raised platform on which to sleep, and a view of the pool for contemplation. The grove would have been silent but for the murmur of prayers, the rustle of robes, the precise chime of a bell calling the disciples to study or meditation, and the hypnotic patter of rain on thatched roofs.

A Tibetan monk caught up with me while I was circumam-bulating the reflecting pool. He was exceptionally tall, power-fully built, and had a broad, flat face.

'Is it true', he whispered, his face twisted with incomprehen-sion, 'that Christians eat the flesh of their god, and drink his blood?'

'Some do. There is a ceremony in which bread and wine are transformed into the body and blood of their Lord and the followers consume them. It is called communion.'

'It is barbaric,' he said, and quickly bowed and turned on his heel.

To escape the confines of the Bamboo Grove, the Buddhists would frequently take to the hills around Rajagriha and satiate their wanderlust.

The association of summits with heavenly abodes or sacred precincts is, of course, universal. Shiva and Parvati reside on Mount Kailas; the ancient Greeks conceived of Olympus as the home of the gods; and Zion is 'the mountain where God loves and will ever love to dwell' (Psalm 68:16). The angels spoke to Moses on Mount Sinai; Mohammed preached his last sermon atop the Mount of Mercy; and Christ was transfigured on Mount Tabor. For the Buddha's part, he delivered his 'Perfection of Wisdom' sutras on a hill outside of Rajagriha known as Gridhra-kuta or 'Vulture Peak'.

The path which twisted up Gridhrakuta was marked with prayer flags, mounds of prayer stones and, courtesy of the Arch-aeological Survey of India, some bubble-gum-pink stair railing. There were rusty plaques posted along the way, commemor-ating scenes from the life of the Buddha. I paused where Deva-datta, a cousin of the Buddha, in a scene not unlike the parable of Cain and Abel but without the fatal consequences, hurled a rock at the Lord in a fit of envy (it only grazed him). Nearby was the site of the former monastery where the Buddha was treated for his wounds. Further on, King Bimbisara had dis-missed his entourage so as to be alone with the Master. They were millennia-old stations etched into the hillside, and they formed a sacred, serpentine geography.

Three Tibetan monks, hardened by Himalayan peaks, strode by me effortlessly; otherwise, I didn't come upon any other pil-grims. I tried to imagine the Buddha climbing the path and in his wake a winding procession of yellow-robed followers with their heads bowed and minds alert in anticipation of a fresh sermon.

Gridhrakuta struck me as less a peak than a spur, but in the sharp crags and jagged rock I could make out, with a little imagination, the beak and spread wings of a vulture. At the summit there was a broad platform and the brick foundations of two Gupta-period temples. Apart from a diminutive altar, at which the Tibetan monks were offering flowers and chanting, the place was bare and unadorned. To deliver the abstract and transcendental message of 'Perfect Wisdom' contained in the *Heart Sutra*, the Buddha had chosen a setting of exposed and uncompromising rock under an expansive sky. The sutra reads, appropriately enough, like an ode to emptiness:

> Here, O Sariputra, form is emptiness, and the very emptiness is form; emptiness does not differ from form, form does not differ from emptiness; whatever is form, that is emptiness, whatever is emptiness, that is form. The same is true of feelings, perceptions, impulses, and consciousness . . .
>
> Therefore, O Sariputra, it is because of his indifference to any kind of personal attainment that a Bodhisattva, through having relied on the perfection of wisdom, dwells without thought-coverings. In the absence of thought-coverings he has not been made to tremble, he has overcome what can upset, and in the end he attains to Nirvana.

The *Heart Sutra* ends with the mantra: 'Gone, Gone, Gone beyond, Gone altogether beyond, O what an awakening, All Hail!'

I, of course, hadn't got beyond anything. I was still struggling with meditation, and the wry, inverted wordplay of the Buddhist texts, but on Vulture Peak there was a glimmer. 'Form is emptiness, emptiness is form . . .' With everything devoid of a separate, independent self, there arises an inextricable union of all things.

At that moment, sitting between stone and sky in contemplation, I was just about sure of it.

It was at Vulture Peak that the *sangha* convened soon after the Buddha's death when the 'Lamp of Wisdom had been blown out by the wind of impermanence'. The gathering is known as the First Council and its purpose was to thrash out a Buddhist Canon from the multifarious sermons and utterances of the Lord. Buddhism was then still an oral tradition, and the most venerable disciples recited the teachings which they had committed to memory. Upali reaffirmed the *Vinaya-pitaka*, which outlined the rules of discipline of the Order; Aranda delivered the *Sutta-pitaka*, the Sermons or Teachings of the Buddha; and Kassapa recited the teachings on metaphysics and philosophy known as the *Abhidhamma-pitaka*. At each successive Council, the three *Pitakas*, or 'Baskets' of the Canon, would be recited, their authenticity and orthodoxy confirmed, and so the tradition perpetuated. It was not until about 25 BC that the Canon was finally written down in Pali, or, more precisely, etched with a metal stylus on dried palm leaves. By then, however, there was already a breach in Buddhist doctrine, and the Pali Canon was by no means universally accepted. The breach grew into a schism which survives to this day.

The division between Hinayana Buddhism ('The Little Vehicle'), practised in Sri Lanka and most of South East Asia, and Mahayana Buddhism (the self-proclaimed 'Greater Vehicle'), observed in Tibet, China, Korea, Mongolia and Japan, can be traced to Vulture Peak. Hinayana sects, such as the Theravada or 'Doctrines of the Elders', hold fast to the Pali Canon and the historical figure of the Buddha. It is Buddhism at its most elemental and austere. Enlightenment is to be attained for oneself alone and by strict observance of the Rules. Mahayana Buddhism emerged in the first century BC as a revolt against the excessive rigidity of the traditional doctrines and practices which were soon to be

laid down in the Pali Canon. The figure of the historical Gautama
faded and was superseded by a soup of esoteric doctrines
and a more catholic Canon, which included an ahistorical,
absolutist Amitabha Buddha, or the 'Buddha of Infinite Light'.
To achieve enlightenment, the Mahayana Buddhist focuses on
faith, merit, and compassion. Unlike the solitary figure of the
Hinayana adept earnestly working out his and only his way to
Nirvana, the followers of the Mahayana School work and pray
for the salvation of all humankind.

The Hinayana accuse their schismatic brothers of heresy and
of butchering the pure teachings of the Master. The latter
usually respond with condescension. Hinayana, they say, is not
so much false as limited. It is based on common doctrines which
the Buddha preached to common disciples. According to
Mahayana texts, when the Master preached his 'Perfection of
Wisdom' sutras on Vulture Peak, his audience was confined to
a select group of enlightened beings.

Clearly, the notion of form as emptiness and emptiness as
form was not meant to be grasped by any old follower, least of
all me.

I got talking with the Tibetan monks on Vulture Peak (Mahayana Buddhists, incidently, with a Canon all their own). They
were on pilgrimage, down from their monastery in Dharamsala.
They had leathery faces and intelligent eyes. I listened to their
laments over Tibet and a life of exile. They believed, perhaps
naïvely, that one day they and their people, led by the Dalai Lama,
would return to Lhasa to restore their monasteries, their culture,
their whole downtrodden Buddhist world. I admired their
resilience.

When I happened to mention that I lived in Spain, the eldest
of the monks suddenly nodded his head and whispered, 'Saint
Teresa of Avila, she knew Nirvana'.

The two of us descended Vulture Peak discussing the

similarities between Buddhist meditations and Saint Teresa's four ways of prayer. Then I took out one of my notebooks and recited to him as we walked. It was a passage from Saint Teresa's 'The Prayer of Quietness', but the words could so easily have been attributed to the Buddha:

> We begin to lose our cravings for things of this earth; and no wonder, because one sees clearly that no riches, no power, no honours, no pleasures, can for a moment, even for the twinkling of an eye, give such true joy.

The monk was in bliss.

At Patna, the murderous capital of Bihar and Ashoka's former capital of Pataliputra, the Ganges was sluggish and the colour of rust. I went off in search of the remains of the legendary Mauryan Empire and found an excavation site with some scant remains of a hall and exactly one sandstone pillar. At the Patna Museum, said to possess a fine collection of Tibetan *thangkas* scroll paintings, the door was bolted and the watchman shrugged and bobbed his head. I spent the afternoon in the Khuda Bhaksh Oriental Library poring over Persian manuscripts and Mogul miniatures, and the night in a dismal hotel close to Saif Khan's Mosque. I was awakened before first light by the urgent, high-pitched call of the *muezzin*.

The seven o'clock bus to Gorakhpur heaved out of the Patna station fully loaded at nine-thirty sharp. I sat beside a pear-shaped man and his emaciated wife. They never spoke to one another, nor to me. She silently fed him a series of pungent dishes from a tiffin. He ate and belched. Ahead lay two flat tyres, three police controls (searching for 'miscreants'), and dozens of prolonged stops in countless villages for no apparent reason whatever. All the while, the sun beat down on the bus and turned the interior into an inferno. It reminded me of Mohammed's comment on travel: 'A journey is a fragment of Hell.' I regretted not having walked.

At Gorakhpur, I just managed to catch the bus to Kushinagara. The driver had bloodshot eyes and grey skin. He was in a hurry. After dark, he told me, it was suicide to be on the road. He gestured as if to slit his throat. We raced to Kushinagara, the horn blaring incessantly at obstacles real and imagined.

I was drawn to the Linh-Son Chinese Temple in Kushinagara by the sound of chanting, the smell of Asian cooking, and the sight of what looked to be very tidy and comfortable quarters for pilgrims. The temple was a curious composite of multi-coloured domes and spires, friezes and balustrades, pillars and niches, rendered in concrete and tile. In the courtyard there were well-tended borders of marigolds and a white marble statue of Kwan-Yin, a figure of mercy in Buddhist mythology whom the Chinese esteem in the way pious Catholics revere the Madonna.

I was greeted at the gate by Tri Thuan, the young *bhikkuni*-in-charge. She wore a starched grey robe and bore three small round scars on top of her shaven head where the sticks of incense had burned into her pate during her ordination ceremony.

'May the Buddha bless you!' she cried, and then led me silently to a room of unaccustomed spotlessness.

Later, we ate dinner together. There were no other monks or nuns; apart from the two local men who helped with the domestic chores, she was alone. When I asked her if she was afraid of being alone in remote Kushinagara, she responded: 'If I am not afraid of death, what have I to fear?'

She was not Chinese, but Vietnamese, from a small village outside Hue. In 1975 she said goodbye to her decimated homeland and what was left of her family, boarded a boat in the night, and fled across the South China Sea. She landed in the

Philippines, found shelter in a refugee camp, and eventually made her way to a new life in a small town in Michigan. The story then cut to her ordination, years of study and prayer, and her mission to the land of the Buddha. Her superior must have observed her iron will and seen the ideal candidate to resurrect the Chinese Temple in Kushinagara. He sent her alone.

When Tri Thuan had arrived eight years before, the temple, built in the 1950s and shortly thereafter abandoned, was hidden beneath a tangle of vines. There was no water, no light, and squatters. She hacked away the vegetation, swept out the temple and oversaw its restoration. She built a house for the squatters, a school, and a pilgrim shelter.

After dinner, she marched me outside to an adjacent field and showed me where the new clinic would go up. She then excused herself; she had work to do.

I slumped off to bed feeling slothful, indecisive and wholly inadequate.

The Buddha died in a grove of sal trees in Kushinagara at the ripe age of eighty; the cause of death, food poisoning. If, as most Buddhist scripture suggests, the Buddha foresaw and planned his passing away in Kushinagara, then his death was a final, determined act of humility. Unlike Patna or Rajagriha, both of which had been thriving capitals, Kushinagara was and always has been a backwater. The disciples thought the place an unfitting scene for the Lord's Great Passing; the Buddha, however, found it ideal. If everything is conditioned by impermanence, what better place from which to enter Nirvana than a village in the boondocks?

The Buddha's last words to his brethren contained a declaration and an imperative: 'Decay is inherent in all component things! Work out your own salvation with diligence.'

The wake lasted seven days. The corpse, perfumed and

covered with garlands of flowers, was then cremated and the ashes divided into eight parts and distributed to the Rajas of the surrounding kingdoms. *Stupas* were built to enshrine the relics and before long these became the focus of cult-like worship. Never mind that the Buddha would have been the first to condemn such displays of reverence; it was too late. Upon the death of the Exalted One, Buddhism was transformed from a moral philosophy into a religion.

I walked to the Nirvana Temple just before dawn. There was no moon and Kushinagara was as black as a void. Someone was fanning the embers of a fire in front of a hovel and wheezing. A Brahman cow stood in the middle of the track.

The gate to the temple compound was locked, so I went over the wall. I made my way through a maze of brick ruins towards the flickering candlelight which shone from the interior of the temple. There was a night watchman curled up and snoozing behind one of the pillars of the portico. I tiptoed past and found myself before a recumbent figure of the Buddha, its gilt glowing brilliantly in the candlelight.

The statue, approximately twenty feet in length and carved from a single block of sandstone, took up most of the temple. It depicted the Buddha reclining on his right side with his face turned towards the west. It was mounted on a stone pedestal carved with now indistinct human figures and inscriptions. There were flowers scattered around the pedestal, and sticks of incense and candles. The statue was draped in a tawdry gold sheet; I gave it a tug and the material slipped off the Buddha and fell to the marble floor silently. The figure was highly stylized. The folds of the Buddha's robes, uniform and sharp, were carved like furrows over an elongated, slender body. The face was finely chiselled and polished and bore an expression of quiet resignation. Here, I thought, was death without agony and torment.

Compared to Christ's agonizing end on the Cross, the Buddha's Great Passing while lying in repose beneath a pair of flowering sal trees was placid, if not painless.

Pilgrims have often commented that the Nirvana Temple is a place of melancholy and sorrow, but I didn't experience any of it. I sat in the golden candlelight at the foot of the Buddha and found the scene altogether uplifting; blissful, a Buddhist might say.

> The traveller has reached the end of the journey! In the freedom of the Infinite he is free from all sorrows, the fetters that bound him are thrown away, and the burning fever of life is no more.
> *Dhammapada*

Just as I was getting to grapple with my own fetters, the night watchman appeared and tossed me out with a harangue in Hindi.

But I went back again and again over the course of some alert, spirit-filled days in Kushinagara. The Nirvana Temple became my refuge (and the night watchman my friend). I spent long hours on the cool, marble floor contemplating the image of the Buddha poised for Nirvana. I read; I meditated; I struggled with demons; I tried to shed the old husk; and I wondered just how I would manage to work out my salvation with diligence. 'Seek ye first the kingdom of God and his righteousness,' said Christ, 'and all these things shall be added unto you.' The Buddha would have agreed.

I wanted to go to just one more place: to Lumbini, the birthplace of Siddhartha Gautama, nestled in the verdant grasslands of the Nepalese Terai. It is the Buddhist Bethlehem, the scene of the Nativity, the site where an infant, whom astrologers had foretold might one day rule the world, was born in a grove of blossoming sal trees. And Tri Thuan, as it happened, was going my way.

This indefatigable *bhikkuni* was not only doing an admirable job of running the Chinese Temple and pilgrim shelter, administering the school, and planning the future clinic in Kushinagara, she was also breaking ground for a temple in Lumbini. She was off to oversee the work, she told me. If I wanted to join her, I was welcome. I glanced at her shiny new Land Cruiser parked inside the temple compound and didn't think twice.

Before setting off the next morning in darkness, Tri Thuan blessed the Buddha Mobile with a prayer and a bow. Now, we were utterly impregnable. We drove to Gorakhpur, turned north for Nepal, and crossed the border just as the mist was rising to reveal a distant horizon of Himalayan peaks white and crystalline with eternal snows. We passed fields of sugar cane and mango groves, and dull, dung-coloured villages where the locals now bore the wider, flatter countenances of Himalayan peoples. The landscape was etched with rivers and water channels fed by the mountains. I spotted white egrets and flamingos, kingfishers and plovers, and water buffalo delighting in a bath.

By mid-morning we were in Lumbini. In the car-park, an enormous sign, rusted and peeling, displayed the ambitious plans of the Lumbini Development Project, which included a sprawl of shops, banks, hotels, a golf course, and, of course, new temples and a nature sanctuary. At the moment, however, there was a conspicuous lack of activity; a handful of tattered merchants were selling the usual trinkets, and some dogs were rolling in the dust.

I went with Tri Thuan to pray in the sacred grove. The precinct was surrounded by a mean barbed-wire fence. Inside, there was a sunken pool where Maya is said to have bathed Siddhartha after his birth, a truncated Ashokan pillar surrounded by a dilapidated Victorian railing, and a corrugated-tin shed that covered the ruins of the ancient temple which marked the precise spot of the birthplace of the Lord. All told, the grove was a picture of neglect, and contrasted wildly with the beatific scene described in early Buddhist texts:

> . . . here was a pleasure-grove of sal-trees, called Lumbini Grove. And at this particular time this grove was one mass of flowers from the ground to the topmost branches, while amongst the branches and flowers hummed swarms of bees of the five different colours, and flocks of various kinds of birds flew about warbling sweetly. Throughout the whole of Lumbini Grove the scene resembled the Cittalaka Grove in Indra's paradise, or the magnificently decorated banqueting pavilion of some potent King. *Jataka*

Tri Thuan prayed and lit candles at the foot of the Ashokan pillar. I sat under a banyan tree to read, but I was soon surrounded by a pack of village boys. They were from one of the five villages that the Lumbini Development Project had obliterated from the landscape. They spent their days scrambling up and down the brick ruins of *stupas* and temples, throwing debris into the sacred pool, and begging from a steady stream of well-to-do Buddhist pilgrims. We had a brief, distressing exchange.

'Where are you from, sir?' one of them asked.

'America.'

'You will take us to *Merica* with you, sir?'

'Ah, but what would your mothers say?'

'Nothing.'

The site of Tri Thuan's future Chinese Temple lay down a dirt track about a mile from the grove. The LDP planners had thoughtfully lined the road with memorial sal trees, but the locals, desperate for firewood, had stripped the branches clean. There were colossal earth-moving machines rusting in a ditch near a long-extinguished, eternal-flame monument to the Buddha. Temples were going up everywhere. Most of the Buddhist nations had each staked out their lot in the dull plain. Tri Thuan's site was across a dirt track from the Korean Temple and next door to the Vietnamese. The Burmese and Japanese were raising temples on shifting marshland just through the woods.

We had a picnic in Tri Thuan's lot; it was full of weeds and surrounded by a shabby cinder-block wall.

'Isn't it beautiful?' she said, blind to the desolation on account of the terrain's spiritual significance.

'Yes,' I said.

She proceeded to pace about the lot measuring the sites of the future temple, clinic, school and pilgrim shelter. I didn't have the slightest doubt that they would all go up in record time.

When we said good-bye, I gave Tri Thuan a bundle of notes. I'd never given to a more worthy cause.

The Korean Temple resembled an American-style budget motel without the cars, but every bit as painfully out of place in the landscape. The grey-robed *bhikkus* and *bhikkunis*, however, were fanatically courteous. I was ushered by a bowing young novice to a spacious room. Later, I dined on pickled vegetables, seaweed and rice with the resident monks and nuns.

No one spoke English, but one of the monks carried an English–Korean pocket translator. I tapped out a string of words which more or less described my condition: PILGRIMAGE . . . MEDITATION . . . PRAYER . . . BLISS . . . KIDNAPPING . . . PANIC . . . FREE . . . LAST STOP LUMBINI. The Korean translations were read aloud and everyone looked my way and alternately nodded or smiled or grimaced as each word prescribed. 'Bliss' elicited blissful gazes; 'kidnapping' caused their faces to twist up in horror. The monk

then entered a message for me: JAPANESE . . . MONK . . .
MURDERED . . . WALKING . . . LUMBINI . . .
DANGER. And this in the birthplace of the Exalted One, the
Light of Asia, the Greatest of the Sons of Men.

In the morning, I hired what appeared to be a British-era
bicycle with the dim intention of out-pedalling potential
trouble.

The Koreans kept a merciless schedule. A gong sounded at
three in the morning calling the resolute to an hour of prayer,
followed by two hours of meditation, and finally a six o'clock
breakfast of seaweed and tea. I conformed religiously, although I
did nod off on occasion during the prayers. I found the chanting
hypnotic, and then someone would strike a wooden bell and
rouse me from my slumber. I followed the litany and watched
the *bhikkus* and *bhikkunis* prostrate themselves before three
images of the Buddha. The ceiling was decked in coloured
lanterns and the air was thick with incense.

TZU KUEI I FU TANG YUAN CHUNG SHENG
(I take refuge in Buddha, wishing all sentient beings)

T'I CHIEH TA TAO FA WU SHANG HSIN
(to understand the great Doctrine and make the superlative
 resolve.)

TZU KUEI I FAH TANG YUAN CHUNG SHENG
(I take refuge in Dharma, wishing all sentient beings)

SHEN JU CHING TSANG CHIH HUI JU HAI
(to penetrate the *Sutta Pitaka* with wisdom as unfathomable as the
 ocean.)

TZU KUEI I SENG TANG YUAN CHUNG SHENG
(I take refuge in Sangha, wishing all sentient beings)

T'UNG LI TA CHUNG I CH'IEH WU AI
(to harmonize multitudes in general, without any obstruction
   whatsoever,)

HO NAN SHENG CHUNG
(and to respect the sacred Sangha.)

In meditation, the Koreans were very strict. I tried my best to
keep up, but often I couldn't help but listen to the sounds of life
waking outside in the early morning hours before dawn. There
was buzzing, and howling, and wild dogs barking, and birds, and
someone dragging their feet along the dirt path and hacking in
the dark. I engaged in a discursive meditation on impermanence.

Throughout the blistering blue days I explored the countryside
for ruins and sought out high ground in the hopes of catching a
glimpse of the Himalayas. I watched some boys, brown and
limber, fishing on a riverbank with bamboo poles and
dragonflies for bait. I passed some villagers as they knelt and
bowed towards Mecca; others I observed making offerings at a
Devi shrine. Local Buddhists, however, were nowhere to be
seen, just foreign pilgrims among the ruins.

Lamentably, I also saw my share of old men, sick men,
corpses and ascetics. In all the centuries that had rolled past since
the Buddha's death, nothing, in fact, had changed.

Before leaving Lumbini, I rode out to Kapilavastu and
wandered around the ruins of the palace where the Buddha is said
to have grown up surrounded by bounty and beauty. I stood in
the threshold of the eastern gate, the so-called Gate of the Great
Departure. Here, I thought, was a site more worthy of reverence
than the Lumbini Grove. When I read the tales of the Buddha's
birth, of how he stepped from his mother's womb, walked seven
paces in each direction and proclaimed, 'I am the only lord in

heaven and earth; from this time forth my births are finished,' I was delighted, but unmoved. The supreme drama, I believed, occurred at Kapilavastu. A prince leaves his palace, his family, and the pleasures of the court. He trades silken robes for the rags of a beggar and goes out into the night in search of the end of life's suffering. It is called the Great Renunciation. It was an act committed by a man guided not by divine prophecy or the caprice of astrologers, but rather by pure reason and compassion. To me, it made all the difference.

4 / The Way of Saint James

Give me my scallop-shell of quiet,
My staff of faith to walk upon,
My scrip of joy, immortal diet,
My bottle of Salvation,
My gown of glory (hope's true gage),
And thus I'll take my pilgrimage.
  Sir Walter Raleigh

'Only fools and fanatics make the pilgrimage at this time of year,'
said the priest with a look of undisguised glee. We were standing
in the courtyard of the Monastery of Roncesvalles on the southern slope of the Spanish Pyrenees. It was the dawn of an early
November day; frost covered the cobblestones and ice had
formed on the fountain where pilgrims stop to slake their thirst.
As the priest spoke, his breath emerged in billowing plumes. 'In
the mountains of Leon, you will freeze to death.'

'All the more reason for a proper benediction,' I said.

He mumbled something incoherent and went off reluctantly
in search of a Roman collar to perform the rite.

I was setting off on the Way of Saint James, a medieval pilgrimage path which crosses the northern breadth of the Iberian
peninsula on its nearly 500-mile westward march to Santiago
de Compostela, where the remains of Saint James, the son of
Zebedee and Salome, are said to rest in the cathedral crypt.
During the summer months, there are thousands of pilgrims
in progress to what is, after Jerusalem and Rome, Christendom's

most venerated pilgrimage site, but in the last fortnight only
two had passed through Roncesvalles. It would be, as I had
hoped, a solitary journey.

Roncesvalles had no grand cloister or rarefied medieval
library. The canons made neither wine nor fruit liqueur, nor
were they known for Gregorian plainsong. And while the overall
architectural scheme of the monastery complex was medieval, its
original grace and uniformity had been dissipated by successive
architectural interventions, most of them indelicate. What
Roncesvalles did possess was a long and noble history stretching
back to the twelfth century of offering refuge and succour to
pilgrims who came over the Pyrenees from France and points
further north on their way to Santiago. The eleven canons who
live at Roncesvalles bear the title of *hospitalero*, or 'one who
offers hospitality'.

I knelt in the chancel of the monastery's Gothic church to re
ceive the benediction. An expansive, stone baldachin rose above
the altar and a rather garish gold, silver and jewel-studded
statue of the Virgin of Roncesvalles, Queen of the Pyrenees, and
protector of shepherds. The morning light barely illuminated the
stained-glass windows in the apse and the church was dark and
dank. The priest stood above me, placed his right hand on my
head, and recited a prayer that hadn't changed, either in spirit or
in letter, for the better part of a millennium:

Oh God, who led your servant Abraham from the city of Ur,
guarding him during all his pilgrimage, and you who were the guide
of the Hebrew people through the desert, we ask you to protect
this your servant who, for the love of Your name, journeys to
Compostela. Be for him a companion on the march, a guide at the
crossroads; give him strength when he is weak, defence in the midst
of danger, shelter along the route, shade from the sun, light in the
darkness, solace in moments of discouragement and firmness in his

purpose . . . May the benediction of God the All-Powerful, Father, Son, and Holy Spirit, descend upon you. Amen.

I walked out of Roncesvalles and into the valley under a brilliant autumnal sky. A line of ash trees and pines formed an orderly, diminishing vista on the road leading south. If my calculations were correct, I would arrive in Santiago de Compostela in a month, just short of the time that the Lord Jesus wandered the wilderness tempted by the devil, lodged with the beasts and ministered to by angels.

The valley was full of tales of apparitions of the Virgin, of pilgrims delivered from darkness and peril, of sacred springs and hallowed mounts, but the hoariest legend of all was more infamous, and at the same time, more poetic.

It was through here in 778 that Charlemagne marched home with his Frankish troops and knights after seven long years of slaying Moors in Iberia. They were fresh from the siege of Pamplona. As the army limped north, the rearguard, led by Roland, was cut off in the valley and slain to a man by Basque warriors. The episode became an epic, the *Chanson de Roland*, but the anonymous twelfth-century author, for reasons of Christian zeal or sheer literary flourish, substituted a vast army of Saracens for the Basques.

So died the soldier of Charlemaine,
With words or weapons, to preach, or fight,
A champion ever of Christian right,
And a deadly foe of the infidel.
God's benediction within him dwell!

In Burguete, the first village I passed, a stooped, black-clad widow gave me a fine oak walking stick. She was sitting in front of her house basking in the warm morning sun. Her ankles were swollen and her legs bulging with veins. She had no more use for the stick. Watching the pilgrims file past, she told me, gave her the sensation of walking, if only vicariously.

In medieval iconography, the pilgrim always carries a staff, along with a scallop shell with which to drink. He wears a floppy hat, a voluminous cape, and sandals. To don medieval garb would have been, well, just a bit too arch, but a walking stick would be useful in fording streams, descending rocky slopes, and threatening wild dogs.

The Way diverged from the road and led to open pastures and woodland. The air smelled of fallen leaves, wood smoke, harvested fields and manure. I passed grazing cows and flocks of sheep, and listened to a shepherd shouting clipped commands to his dog in *Euskera*, the Basque's anomalous native tongue. I heard the gunshots of hunters out for hare and pheasant.

The path was marked with yellow arrows painted on stones, tree trunks, bridges, sign posts, gates and walls. I also carried a pilgrim's guide which contained maps of considerable detail. Still, at midday, I stood in a hillock pasture having momentarily lost the trail. A farmer and his son were pulling Cyclopean boulders from the field; they were sweating profusely beneath their *bonetas*, a wider version of the French beret. I approached them to ask the way. They conversed in *Euskera*, pointed to a distant break in the woods, and returned to their labours without another word. I followed a narrow path for about half an hour, but came to a halt in the midst of a thicket. I cursed the toiling farmer and his son. I retraced my steps. I made a slow, methodical search of the periphery of the pasture. At last, I caught sight of a yellow ribbon fluttering from a sapling at a break in the stone wall. I had lost precious time. The sun was already on the descent.

I pressed on past Mezquiriz, Ureta, Viscarret and Linzoain. At

dusk, I was ascending a steep mountain path leading through a
dense forest of pines. Enormous shadows, tilting down from the
treetops, obscured the way. If it had been summer, I would have
had hours yet of daylight, but now, in November, as a distant
church bell tolled six o'clock, it was night. Progress was slow. I
stumbled on rocks and logs and caught my trousers on brambles.
I shuffled ahead, poking my walking stick as I went. Were it not
for an ample moon, I would surely have been lost. The sky was
luminous. I could clearly make out scores of constellations,
among them Pegasus, the curse horse.

When I at last spied the lights of Zubiri gleaming in the
valley, I uttered a brief prayer to Santiago and the Virgin of
Roncesvalles to boot.

The interior of the bar Gau Txori (appropriately enough,
'Night Bird') seemed darker than the night from which I was
seeking refuge. A cloud of tobacco smoke, acrid and dense, hung
over the room. In a corner, a group of men were playing *mus*,
slapping down faded playing cards stamped with images of cups,
swords, clubs and kings. They anted up, bluffed and wagered in
Euskera. A television blared in Castilian.

The bar was run by three Basque brothers. They all had
high cheekbones, deep-set eyes and aquiline noses. Ignacio, the
youngest, served me a plate of white beans and chorizo,
and heady red wine. I asked him where I might pass the
night.

'There are a number of hostels in town,' he explained, 'but if
you are a pilgrim, and I imagine you are, for only a pilgrim
would venture across Spain at this time of year, then you are free
to sleep in the old schoolhouse. But first, you must obtain the
key from the mayor.'

It was getting late and I told Ignacio that I feared rousing the
good *alcalde*.

'Well, I happen to know that the mayor is never in bed at this hour; you see, I am his son.'

He went to fetch the key while I sipped my wine.

The old schoolhouse was crumbling; windows were shattered; and there were swallows nesting in the rafters. The building was divided into two large rooms, one marked *Niños*, the other *Niñas*. I lit a candle and found a confusion of furniture, text books, boxes and paper strewn about the floor. There were miniature desks, each with its own ink well and blotter, a graffiti-covered blackboard, and yellowed maps. A large portion of Morocco still appeared as a Spanish colony. I unrolled my sleeping bag on the bare wood floor. In the unsteady candlelight, chattering with cold, I began the first entry in my journal: 'Only fools and fanatics make the pilgrimage at this time of year . . .' I had no desire to conform to either label.

The sensation upon waking at the first dawn of my pilgrimage was not one of spiritual renewal, but the excruciating and altogether worldly aches of long-idle muscles and joints. I winced as I turned over in my sleeping bag, at once aware of the minor but multiple bruises from my nocturnal bumbling in the woods. The floor of the schoolhouse was cold and hard, something which the wine had obscured the night before. A diffuse light entered through frost-covered windows; only where the panes were shattered did the light advance in long, radiant streams. Gusts of wind sent papers fluttering and dust rising. I rose and washed in the numbing water from a spigot outside. I was struck by what had previously been a vague notion, that of penance.

I lumbered out of Zubiri bound for Pamplona. Everything looked leaden despite the brilliant light. On the edge of town, an enormous magnesium plant spewed steam, smoke and a debilitating stench. There were graffiti everywhere. The most common scrawls were *Gora ETA!* ('Long Live ETA!'), in reference to the

Basque terrorist group, and *Españoles Fuera!*, or 'Spaniards Out!'
I also came upon some anti-clerical musing. On a sign indicating
the *Camino de Santiago*, as the Way is known in Spanish, someone had painted *Es una mentira!* ('It's a lie!').

The derisive graffito was, in fact, only a crude manifestation of
a centuries-old debate that calls into question the authenticity of
the pilgrimage. Like the Shroud of Turin, fragments and nails of
the True Cross, saintly visions, sacrosanct relics, hallowed
shrines, or indeed anything smacking of the miraculous, the
pilgrimage to Santiago de Compostela has its detractors. Their
incredulousness is not altogether unfounded. What the faithful
regard as a revelation, sceptics consider pure legend. The story,
whether fact or fiction, goes something like this:

St James, the Apostle, brother of St John (Jesus gave the two
the title of *Boanerges*, or 'Sons of Thunder'), was one of Christ's
most immediate followers. When the Apostles set out from
Galilee to evangelize the fledgling creed, James is said to have
made his way to distant Iberia. After sowing the seed of the
Christian faith, he returned to Jerusalem, and in A D 44 became
the first martyr among the Apostles.

> It was at this same time that Herod exerted his authority to
> persecute some of those who belonged to the Church. James, the
> brother of John, he beheaded, and then, finding that this was
> acceptable to the Jews, he went further, and laid hands on Peter
> too. *Acts 12:1–3.*

That much is documented in Scripture. Thereafter, however,
the story gets somewhat fanciful. James's disciples stowed their
master's remains on a ship (some insist it was made of stone)
bound for the Iberian peninsula. They landed on the Atlantic
coast of present-day Galicia at a spot known as Finisterre, or
'World's End'. The Apostle was buried in a crypt and abandoned

to oblivion. Some eight centuries later, a hermit received a vision of a star illuminating a spot on an isolated vale in the interior of Galicia. The vision was promptly interpreted as a divine sign; the site was excavated, a crypt discovered, and the remains attributed to St James. On the spot a church was built and a city born, Santiago de Compostela (*campo de la estrella*, or 'field of the star').

Whether or not St James's bones actually lie in the cathedral crypt at Santiago is, I believe, superfluous. I tend to agree with historians who suppose that the cult of St James evolved as a rallying cry against the Moorish invaders of Iberia. The Saracens went into battle believing that they were protected by the arm of Mohammed. The Christians, in turn, looked to the Apostle for inspiration. *Santiago el Matamoros* or 'St James the Moor Slayer' became a popular moniker for the Apostle, and on occasion he was sighted mounted on a white steed, leading the Christian armies into battle.

What *is* indisputable is the historical and spiritual reality of the Way itself. During the Middle Ages, untold millions made the journey south from every corner of the Continent and the British Isles, over the Pyrenees and across Iberia to Santiago. They were exposed to disease, highway robbery, battles between Moorish and Christian armies, false prophets and swindlers, but still they ventured forth, seeking penance, invoking prayers, paying homage, and gaining questionable indulgences at the tomb of St James. The vast sea of pilgrims included the pious and the irreverent, popes and paupers, scholars and simpletons, saints and charlatans, fortune seekers and common criminals (the last were frequently sentenced to march to Santiago in an example of innovative medieval jurisprudence). The Way of St James became, rather unintentionally, one of the most cosmopolitan itineraries in all of Europe. Hospices, churches, shrines, convents and monasteries sprang up along the route, and through their thresholds passed Francis of Assisi, El Cid and Jan Van Eyck, to name but three. Along the Way travelled not just pilgrims, but ideas, debate, speculation and art. 'Europe', wrote Goethe 'was formed journeying to Santiago.'

I crossed the Arga river at Larrasoana. Here, the *camino* followed a well-travelled national road where elongated trucks laden with fresh-cut timber from the Pyrenees roared past, leaving me enveloped in dust, sand and roadside debris. There were scores of dead dogs, their carrion putrid and appalling. I crossed the river yet again at the entrance to the hamlet of Iroz and a third time over a stout, medieval bridge whose stones were worn smooth from the cumulative steps of centuries' worth of pilgrims, soldiers, peasants and their livestock. The route was as circuitous as medieval logic, but I was in no hurry. *Ambulare pro Deo*, 'to wander or walk for God', was a tenet of the medieval Church, a call to the faithful to imitate the Lord's journey through the Wilderness. By detaching oneself from the routine and familiar surroundings of domestic life, striking out on the Way, and submitting to hardship and uncertainty in a foreign land, the pilgrim is thrown into a state of intense introspection, reflection and prayer. The pilgrim progresses over a physical landscape, but it is the spiritual journey that counts. It is the Wayless Way of Meister Eckhart, 'where the Sons of God lose themselves and, at the same time, find themselves'.

I entered the industrial outskirts of Pamplona in a fading light. Concrete apartment blocks, empty lots and small factories lined the route. I was eyed with suspicion by passers-by and set upon by a pair of emaciated stray dogs. Just as I was wondering when the more noble Pamplona would appear, I caught sight of the twin towers of the cathedral rising above a Cubist landscape of red-tile roofs. A cobblestone lane led up through a corridor flanked by massive walls and battlements of honey-coloured stone. I crossed a drawbridge whose chains and gears, although dating from the seventeenth century, appeared well oiled and ready for any eventuality. Further on rose the Portal de Francia, crowned by the imperial coat of arms depicting the double-headed eagle, a remnant of the ill-fated and short-lived union of the Castilian and Habsburg domains.

By the time I reached Pamplona cathedral, my stride had been reduced to a shuffle, my feet were in agony, and the weight of my backpack felt as if I were bearing a veritable cross. I submerged my head in the fountain in the square and collapsed to gaze at the Corinthian columns, porticoes and pediments of the cathedral's neo-classical façade. When the bells in the twin towers struck six, the street lamps blinked on; bats emerged from the cracks and hollows in the stone, and I entered a side door in search of a priest.

At Roncesvalles I had been given a document which listed the names of the principal towns along the Way to Santiago. In each town I was obliged to obtain a stamp from the local priest, and so verify my progress along the route. This custom survives from the Middle Ages, when the proof of a completed pilgrimage was a much sought-after currency in the granting and trading of indulgences, and not merely for the pilgrim, but also for the souls of those already in Purgatory. The practice, of course, became rife with abuse, and led to an outcry in the medieval Church against pilgrimages. The detractors were fond of quoting St Augustine, who insisted that not by journeying, but by loving do we draw near to God; to Him who is everywhere present and everywhere entire we approach not by our feet, but by our hearts. Augustine was expressing a sentiment that went back to the Johannine Gospel, according to which God is to be adored neither in Jerusalem nor in Gerizim, but in spirit and truth.

The cathedral was empty but for a handful of stout old women murmuring vespers. A dim light entered through stained glass set in high ogival arches. Some candles flickered. There was a remote scent of incense and damp. In the sacristy, I found an aged priest asleep on a stool. He wore a wrinkled cassock, a stiff Roman collar and a simple wooden crucifix. His hair had the look of spun silver. When I knocked gently at the door, he woke up in mid-sentence. '. . . Advent is a time of joy, brothers and sisters . . . Who in God's name are you?' he shouted.

'A pilgrim.'

'What do you want here?'

'A stamp for my document.'

He stared at me silently through bloodshot eyes. 'How are your feet?' he finally asked.

'Dead.'

'That is the honour of the pilgrim.'

He rummaged through some drawers filled with rosaries and tattered missals, devotional photographs of Paul VI and candle stubs, vials of Holy Water and a fine fossil of a leaf. When he found the stamp, he dabbed it in an antique ink block and pressed it with a trembling hand to my document. The central image was the coat of arms of Pamplona, but it was smeared and illegible.

As I was leaving, he said, 'In the mountains of Leon you will freeze.'

There was no refuge for pilgrims in Pamplona so I roamed the narrow streets of the old quarter in search of a place to sleep. It was the hour in which Spaniards promenade and the lanes were full. The locals had the look of contentment that comes from living in a prosperous provincial capital. They were well dressed and well fed. They walked slowly, greeting friends and passers-by as they went. The shops were busy and crowds were spilling in and out of cafés and bars. No one, I was glad to see, paid me much attention. Why would they? Pilgrims had been wandering the streets of Pamplona for centuries; they were a fixture in the cityscape, transient, but their ranks perpetually renewed.

In the Plaza de la Virgin de la O, I found a modest pension where I took a cramped room beneath the eaves. I managed to wrangle a pilgrim's discount.

'What Pamplona needs is a place to shelter you pilgrims,' said the proprietor. 'If I don't grant you a discount, I am made to feel Godless, and if I do, I lose money. It isn't just. When you get to Santiago, the least you can do is pray for me.'

I would.

Before dropping off to sleep, I read from the *Liber Sancti Jacobi*, also known as the *Codex Calixtinus*, a five-volume tome devoted to the Apostle. Written in 1139 by the French cleric Aymeric Picaud, the fifth volume can be considered Europe's first guide book, a sort of Michelin for the pilgrim, in which the author gives a scrupulous description of what the potential pilgrim could expect to encounter along the Way (bandits, perilous river crossings and barbaric locals) and where he could find the best water, food and lodging.

On the locals hereabouts, Picaud, ever the chauvinist, did not mince his words:

They are a barbarous people, different from all others in customs and disposition, full of evil, of blackness, of ignoble aspect, wicked, perverse, treacherous, disloyal, lewd, drunken, aggressive, ferocious, savage, soulless, damned, impious and rude, cruel and quarrelsome, devoid of any virtue and trained in every vice and iniquity, partners in evil with the Getas and the Saracens, and direct enemies of our Gaulic nation. For a miserable coin, a Navarrese or a Basque would do away with a Frenchman . . . What's more, they give lewd kisses to the vulvas of their women and their mules. For all of this, a person of education can do nothing but reproach the people of Navarra.

How French, I thought. For my part, I was finding the locals to be delightful.

I woke to the sound of rain pelting the tile roof. When I gazed out of the narrow attic window, there were torrents of water overflowing the eaves. Beyond lay a cityscape enveloped in a dull, shadowless fog. This, alas, was the true autumnal scene in northern Spain. The previous days, radiant and genial, had been a kind of blessing.

I left town in a drizzle. The cobblestones were slick and gleaming, but everything else, the storefronts, the sky, the stone of medieval façades, even the faces of the Pamplonese, had turned an insipid grey. The route lay in the shadows of ramparts, bulwarks, and a mighty pentagonal citadel. It was difficult to take a turn without encountering martial architecture. For me, Pamplona had the air of a siege town.

By noon I was climbing Monte el Perdon, or the Mount of Forgiveness. The steep ascent was a penance. The path was strewn with stones and the rain created deep gullies over which I was forced to leap, not always successfully. The storm got worse. Halfway up the slope, I came to Zariquiegui and took refuge in the village church, a Romanesque gem in shocking disrepair. Inside, there was a single nave, a barrel vault, and capitals carved with floral motifs. This was clearly my preference, an earth-bound, humble style far from the pretensions of lofty Gothic and Baroque edifices. In the purity of the Romanesque, prayer and contemplation, I found, came easily. Here was just the sort of spiritual intimacy that I was seeking and which the pilgrimage trail fostered. I prayed for clarity and grace, and I realized, as never before, that I was a soul in need. It was a small but crucial step along the Way.

A village matron came to ring the church bell. After, she invited me to dry my clothes by her fire and to lunch. She lived in a small, stone house just off the square. The front door gave on to a kitchen–sitting room. There was a wide, open hearth with a fire burning. On the mantle was a sepia photograph of a handsome, if unsmiling, young couple which I presumed to be her wedding picture. There was a shrine to the Virgin, a table, a cupboard, and some odd chairs. The kitchen consisted of a stone sink, an ice box, and a coal stove. A shotgun was propped in the corner. I dried my clothes by the fireside and feasted on soup, steak, bread, wine, fruit, coffee and brandy. All the while I tried to engage my hostess in conversation, but she hardly said a word. Only as I was leaving did she suddenly say, 'There are villagers who hide behind their shutters at the sight of a pilgrim, but my grandmother looked after them, as did my mother. It is the least we can do.'

The sky was ashen and heavy, but the rain had stopped. At the summit of Monte el Perdon, the mist cleared to reveal a patchwork of hills, scattered ilex, and the roofs and church towers of Aquiturrain, Uterga and Muruzabal.

At the foot of the mountain, I came upon an old man poised in the middle of the path. He was, it seemed, waiting for me.

'I saw you coming down the path; you are sure-footed, but too slow. At that pace you will never arrive in Santiago.'

'God willing,' I said curtly.

'God's will has little to do with it. Follow me.'

We walked through a landscape of orchards and groves. The branches of the trees were weeping from the weight of ripe fruit. The old man stopped to gather up some fallen apples and offered them to me. 'Don't worry,' he assured me, 'I am not a thief, they are mine.' He kept a brisk pace and I strained to match his gait. He was from the village of Aquiturrain, and like every village along the *camino*, Aquiturrain had its tale of the pilgrimage. This is what he told me:

Sometime in the Middle Ages, Felicia of Aquitaine, the pious

daughter of a noble French family, made the arduous pilgrimage
to Santiago de Compostela. Upon her return, she was so inspired
by the experience that she decided to renounce her title, her possessions, her family, and, indeed, all that was worldly. Henceforth, she lived amidst the poor. She dressed in sack cloth; ate
what food she could beg; slept in a squalid hovel; and engaged
in a life of prayer. To her brother William, Duke of Aquitaine, a
religious life was all very well and good, but such fanaticism
reeked of scandal. He sought out his sister and implored her to
return to the fold. She reminded him, citing Scripture, that, in
fact, she *was* in the fold and would never again return to her
former life of privilege and vanity. The Duke then promptly, and
without warning, stabbed her to death. Soon after, overwrought
with guilt, William travelled to Rome to confess his sin. His penance, appropriately enough, was to follow in his sister's footsteps
to Santiago. The pilgrimage seemed to have struck a similar
chord in the two siblings. William returned from Santiago a
changed man. He stopped in Obanos, a short walk from
Aquiturrain, and took up the life of a penitent hermit. Later,
William would become St William, but Felicia, alas, seems to
have been forgotten by the saint makers in Rome.

I had lost track of the time and the surroundings as the old
man wove his tale. We had passed through Uterga and
Muruzabal and now stood before a simple stone cross on the
outskirts of Obanos. The monument marked the point where
the *camino* from Roncesvalles meets another, lesser-known route
which descends from Somport. There wasn't another pilgrim in
sight.

'Don't ever say that you don't know the tale of Aquiturrain.'
And with that the old man turned and walked back the way we
had come. I bit into one of his apples; it was deep crimson and
succulent.

At dusk, I arrived in Puente la Reina. I was told to knock at the door of the Convento de Los Padres Reparadores (the 'Restoring Fathers'), where, a villager assured me, I would find good shelter. I slept on a stone floor in the convent's dank, cold cellar. No one mentioned dinner, but I was too fatigued to care. I dropped off to sleep and dreamt of bloody William.

At first light, I crossed the Arga river over a twelfth-century bridge of six flawless stone arches. It was pouring with rain. For two days there was scarcely a break in the clouds. I trudged through a landscape of mud shrouded in mist. I took shelter in barns, abandoned shepherds' huts, and under medieval bridges, but I rarely had time to linger. The days were growing shorter.

The rain stopped as I drew near to the vineyards of La Rioja. In Torres del Rio, I came upon a pack of village boys taunting an old man. They called him *loco* (crazy), *un chiflado* (a crackpot), and *tonto de culo* (stupid ass). The man was trying to stutter a reply, but was too worked up to be coherent. When I approached, the boys ran off laughing.

'Sons of the devil!' he finally managed to gasp, but the boys were gone.

I helped him to sit down and regain his composure. He was thin and frail and severely cross-eyed. His name was Ramon Sostres. He was an orphan, an ex-seminarian and a bachelor, who lived alone. He had the habit of taking in pilgrims, whom he referred to as *hijos de Dios*, or 'children of God'. When he offered me a room for the night, I accepted.

We walked to the house in the dark. There were no street lights. When we arrived, I was shocked to discover a grand town house named Casa Santa Barbara. Above the threshold was a ceramic plaque of the Virgin and Child and the inscription *Ave Maria Gratia Plena*. The house, Ramon told me, belonged to a very rich and compassionate lady who lived in Madrid, but she never visited. She allowed Ramon to occupy the house. Inside, the halls, rooms and walls were utterly bare. Ramon led me to a 'pilgrims' shelter' which he had installed in one of the empty salons; it consisted of a number of car seats retrieved from the junk heap and arranged imaginatively on a wet stone floor. My heart sank, but Ramon was beaming with pride.

I invited him to dinner at the local bar. He ate like a man possessed. I think he was actually starving. The bar was full of men. Everyone was watching the television, on which there was a game show featuring scantily clad young women. It was interminable, but Ramon insisted on staying. I drank too much wine.

Weaving home in the dark, Ramon waxed on about the blonde on the game show. 'That is why I left the seminary,' he confessed without warning. 'I am a man. I need to take my liberties.' Even if only by watching television.

I stretched out on the rear seat of a Ford displaced on the floor of the Casa Santa Barbara. I kept hearing voices from upstairs. Ramon had said that he lived alone, but the voices were distinct, some high-pitched, others little more than a murmur. And there was something else; they were speaking Latin.

In the morning, the air was clear and cold, and the sky a violent blue. Ramon didn't have a kitchen, so we walked to the bar for coffee, but it was closed. It was Sunday. There was a gypsy woman sitting in the square. She had a beautiful face and an enormous bell-shaped body. When Ramon greeted her, she stared at her pudgy feet bulging from a pair of shocking-pink bedroom slippers. Otherwise, she was dressed entirely in black. Ramon asked her if she had a fire going and if she would be good enough to give this pilgrim a cup of coffee. She nodded without looking at me, heaved to her feet, and motioned for me to follow her. I bid farewell to Ramon. He got rather emotional and his crossed eyes welled up. 'If I weren't so old, I'd go with you,' he said.

There was just one thing I wanted to know.

'You told me that you lived alone, didn't you?'

'Oh yes, never a woman to hold me down.'

'Last night, I thought I heard voices.'

'But that was only me! I was practising my Latin. These villagers, they are ignorant. I cannot talk to them. They think I am a fool, but I was schooled by Jesuits!'

I hurried after the gypsy as she waddled out of town. From behind me, Ramon called out, *'Domine, dirige nos'* ('Lord, guide us').

She lived in a shanty on a garbage-strewn lot on the edge of the village. Smoke rose from the chimney and seeped out of cracks and holes in the roof and walls. Inside, it was very dark; blankets hung over the windows to keep out the light. When my eyes grew accustomed to the darkness, I found an elderly man and woman sitting on crates around the fire in a room brimming with junk. The walls were covered with images of television stars and expensive cars torn from magazines, a circus poster, another of the Virgin of Guadalupe and a third, faded and sinister, of *El Generalísimo* Francisco Franco.

They were very hospitable. A crate was pulled up for me to sit. While the gypsy women fixed coffee, I tried to engage the man in conversation, but when he opened his mouth, the only thing that came out was spittle. The women giggled and served me coffee in a filthy, germ-encrusted cup. It was no time to be squeamish. I closed my eyes and drank it down. The coffee was thick with sugar and tepid.

The rest of the family, and I gathered it was a substantial brood judging by the sheer quantity of laundry and rags scattered and hung about, was out pruning the grape vines after the harvest. In a few more days they would be gone. They moved around France and Spain according to the harvests, never staying in one place for more than a month at a time. It was a nomadic life; home was the road.

Pilgrims and gypsies share a condition of restlessness. Both are forever arriving and just as quickly departing. To linger means to grow slothful, stagnant, to die.

I walked through the clipped vineyards of La Rioja, crossed a sluggish Ebro river in Logroño, and passed through Navarrete and Najera under radiant skies. At night, the temperature would drop to nearly freezing, but during the day, I walked in shorts and shirt sleeves.

Apart from the much-needed time to reflect, to pray, and to give thanks for a host of blessings, I was also having a wonderful time. My mind was clear, and I was feeling stronger with every day's march. The locals couldn't have been more forthcoming. The food was exceptional and the wine better still. My Spanish was improving. I had ambled around the exquisite Romanesque cloisters in the cathedral at Pamplona and in the Church of San Pedro de la Rua in Estella, marvelled at the Gothic choir carved by the brothers Amutio in Najera, and paused before the sepulchres of kings and the tombs of nameless pilgrims. The Way, I was discovering, was like a Grand Tour, but with a spiritual bent.

Although stern medieval moralists, quoting the likes of St Jerome and St Augustine, were often exhorting their flock to stay at home, warning them that the dangers of a pilgrimage, both physical and spiritual, might very well undo its benefits, the fact remains that undertaking a pilgrimage came to be regarded as a sign of a well-rounded character. Life in the Middle Ages was dark and drab and offered no means of escape, with the exception of marching off to war or setting off on a pilgrimage. In a manual of medieval psychology, John de Burg wrote, *'Contra acediam, opera laboriosa bona ut sunt peregrinationes ad loca sancta.'* ('Against *acediam*, physical labour and pilgrimages to holy places are beneficial.') *Acediam* was that special form of anxiety, weariness of heart, tedium, torpor and apathy which the

Renaissance would rename *melancholia*. Needless to say, legions of adventurous souls eagerly hit the road, fired by open spaces, foreign lands and tales of miracles. Some didn't come back, preferring to live perpetually, as it were, on the hoof. In *Tesoro de la lengua castellana o española* (1611), the cleric and grammarian Sebastian de Covarrubias defined a *bordonero* as 'one who adopts the pilgrim's guise of a cloak and staff [*un bordón*] and goes wandering the land so as not to work. They are a danger to any Republic, and in many places [these men and women] are scrutinized, for often times they are nothing more than illicit lovers, although they say they are husband and wife.'

In the cathedral at Santo Domingo de la Calzada, I found the traces of the original Romanesque church, Gothic embellishments, a Renaissance altarpiece by Damian Forment, a Baroque tower, and the crypt of Santo Domingo, one of the Way's greatest champions and a builder of bridges and hospices along the trail. There was also a crowing cock and a clucking hen in a gilded Gothic cage; the story of how they got there is part of pilgrim lore:

   In the fourteenth century, a young Frenchman named Hugonell was making the pilgrimage to Santiago de Compostela in the company of his parents. At the inn in which they were passing the night in Santo Domingo de la Calzada, a young maid took a fancy to Hugonell and flirted unabashedly with the handsome foreigner. Hugonell, however, was on pilgrimage; his mind was alert, his spirit soaring and his heart pure. He was not thinking of the pleasures of the flesh. Besides, Hugonell found the maid homely. He ignored her. In a fit of unrequited love (or, at least, of pique), the maid accused Hugonell of robbing silver from the till. Medieval justice was swift and merciless; the chief magistrate sentenced the young man to hang. Clemency was denied and the execution promptly carried out. No sooner had

Hugonell stopped kicking on the gallows than his parents heard his voice, clear and sweet, telling them that he was alive thanks to the intervention of St James. They would see each other, he said, in Santiago. His parents made straight for the home of the chief magistrate to tell him that their son was alive and well. The magistrate baulked. 'As alive as this hen and rooster!' he said, pointing to the roasted fowl laid out on his luncheon table. Whereupon the birds leapt to their feet and began to strut across the table. Hugonell's parents proceeded to Santiago, their faith redoubled. The maid was shunned and never married.

I loved these pilgrim tales; they gave the Way a lyrical richness and, like stations of pilgrimage, they grew more compelling, not less so, as the centuries rolled past.

By the time I reached Burgos, the so-called Shield of Castile, El Cid country, and the former provisional capital of Franco's rebellious Movimiento Nacional, I had been on the Way for ten days; my pilgrim's document bore seven seals, and the sky was grey and moving fast with the threat of more rain.

I walked up to the Seminary of San Jeronimo in search of a bed. At the front door, the watchman, a little man with the face of a drinker, waved me away in contempt. There was no place for pilgrims, he told me, and insinuated that I should go back to wherever it was I came from. It was clear that I would have to speak with a priest. I sat down on the entrance steps and waited while the watchman fumed. Presently, a young, vigorous priest came bounding up the steps, his cassock flapping in the wind. He saw that I was waiting and tried to hurry past, but I blocked his ascent.

'Excuse me, Father.'

'What is it?'

'I am a pilgrim looking for shelter for the night.'

'There is no place for you here.'

Now I happened to know that there were precisely eleven seminarians housed in an edifice roughly the size of Versailles. 'But surely there must be some uninhabited corner. I have a sleeping bag. All I really need is a roof over my head.'

'No,' he said, and brushed by me.

This was the first time that anyone had denied me anything along the Way; not that I had ever asked for anything exorbitant, but the courtesy offered pilgrims was virtually universal among the clergy and lay people alike.

I made for the archbishop's residence and knocked on a weighty, iron-studded door, but no one answered.

'What do you want?' came a voice from behind me.

I turned to find a middle-aged priest in a black suit and Roman collar. He was carrying a briefcase. His face was pink and, like those of many priests, exceedingly well shaven.

'Ah, good afternoon, Father. I was hoping that you might be able to direct me to a pilgrim shelter.'

'I cannot.'

'How is it possible that with all the ecclesiastical buildings in Burgos, there is no place for a pilgrim?'

'We have better things to do than look after wanderers.'

'Forgive me, but I am not a wanderer; I am a pilgrim, and I have my document to prove it.'

'I do not care what you have or do not have. There is no place for you here. Go find a hotel.' He began to fiddle with his keys, but I was standing in the doorway and he couldn't get by.

'But what of your Christian duty to shelter those in need?'

No reply.

'I hope that you never find yourself without a place for the night, Father.' I then stepped aside.

As he unlocked the door and crossed the threshold, I had just one more thing to say. 'Hypocri—' but the last syllable was muffled by the slamming of the door.

I checked into a cheap hotel and read St John of the Cross to lift my spirits.

> In darkness, on a night
> Inflamed with love and sweet anxiety,
> O daring! O delight!
> I left – none noticed me –
> My house was yielded to tranquillity.
>
> In darkness, veiled from sight,
> I took the secret stair unerringly,
> O daring! O delight!
> In dark and secrecy,
> My house was yielded to tranquillity.
>
> Upon that night of bliss,
> When none beheld, I parted secretly,
> Nor looked on that or this,
> And nothing guided me
> But light that brimmed my heart so ardently.

In the morning, I set off to explore the cathedral. For days I had been revelling in the humble spirit of the Romanesque; this was the first significant Gothic edifice I had come across along the *camino*. The effect was overwhelming. The cathedral rose unchallenged from the centre of Gothic Burgos, surrounded by medieval town houses, churches and palaces of the same white sandstone which time and pollution had turned the colour of lead. I stood before the western façade and strained to take in the vertical view. Pointed arches, openwork spires, turrets, friezes and crocketed pinnacles all soared heavenward. Only the gargoyles looked down. Every conceivable stone surface was carved, chiselled, polished, weighted and counterbalanced to form a vital element in an improbable, nearly miraculous whole. Despite its accumulated mass, the cathedral appeared to float.

Curiously enough, the architects principally responsible for building what is considered one of Spain's most singular Late Gothic monuments were a Frenchman in the thirteenth century and a German in the fifteenth. The cathedral's founder, bishop Maurice (Mauricio) of Burgos, was an Englishman.

In 1218, Maurice travelled to Paris for the wedding of Fernando III, *El Santo*. When he saw the brilliant white vision of Notre-Dame going up on the Ile de la Cité, Maurice knew at once that a new architecture was being conceived to give form to a new manner of thinking, a new liturgy, a new man. In the Romanesque, the sacred was grasped largely by intuition, but the Gothic compelled the observer to seek out the sacred not only with the spirit, but with the mind. It was an architecture for the times. Scholasticism was creating a revolutionary synthesis between Aristotelian rationalism and Christian thought, and the Gothic was its physical manifestation.

Three years after his encounter with the Gothic in Paris, Maurice was laying the foundation stone of the Burgos cathedral. Not surprisingly, the building took its inspiration from Notre-Dame, albeit on a smaller, more modest scale. Alas, the cathedral's original architectural purity has been eclipsed by later alterations and additions more or less Rococo in character.

Inside the cathedral, I stretched out on a pew and looked up to the dizzying Mudejar cupola. I stood over the funerary stones of El Cid. I climbed and descended the Golden Staircase. I reeled in the Isabeline splendour of the Constable's Chapel; and I snuck into the sacristy for a quick glimpse of Leonardo da Vinci's 'Mary Magdalene'. It was all rather too much. In truth, I longed for the quiet resonance of the Romanesque, the simple nave beneath a barrel vault, and the spirit of an early, humble Church. I longed for the Way.

I walked out of Burgos and into the flat, featureless expanse of the Spanish plateau.

In Carrion de los Condes I encountered a 'pilgrim'. He was a Lebanese sailor named Mickey. He had jumped a Dutch freighter in Barcelona, squandered his money on rum and whores, and set off without a *peseta* along the Way of St James. He was destined for the port of La Coruña in Galicia, where he hoped to sign on with a ship bound for Latin America. Like most sailors, he loathed walking, but he marvelled at the generosity offered to pilgrims. 'I thought I'd seen everything,' he kept repeating, 'but this pilgrimage business is like Utopia!'

We were at the pilgrim shelter at the Church of Santa María. Don José, the parish priest, knew very well that Mickey wasn't a pilgrim, but he took him in anyway. It was, he told me grudgingly, his Christian obligation.

I had dinner with Don José and his sister in the parish house. She was dressed in her bathrobe and slippers, and shuffled between the kitchen and the dining room, serving dinner silently. She was a tragic type common throughout rural Spain – the spinster sister who cares for her priestly brother. When I caught her eye, she seemed to look right through me, unblinking, like a phantom figure.

There was a place set at the table for Mickey, but he didn't turn up. Don José was irate. 'These Bohemians take advantage of Christian charity,' he said, turning red in the face, 'and most of them are not even believers!' He went on to recount how he had taken in a similar man only two days before. 'I took pity on him and gave him a thousand *pesetas*. What did he do? He went out and got drunk and came banging on the door at three o'clock in the morning!'

'It's hard to be selective in charity,' I said.

But Don José wasn't listening, he had turned on the television.

He watched the same inane game show that had so captivated Ramon the week before, and I suspect for the same reasons, although he seemed to prefer a buxom brunette.

When it came time to lock up the church compound for the night, Mickey still hadn't returned. I made the rounds of the town's bars with Don José to look for him. The priest knew where all the bars were, but he wouldn't set foot inside; he sent me instead, while he lurked in the shadows in the street. After searching in about half a dozen establishments, I found Mickey drinking whisky and slurring congenially with some locals. 'Ahhhh, my pilgrim friend,' he said, squinting in the fluorescent light, 'come, I invite you for a drink.'

'It will have to be another time. Father José is waiting, he wants to lock up for the night.'

He cursed, but followed sheepishly.

Outside, Don José had worked himself into a blind rage. When he saw Mickey stumbling out of the bar and into the street, he unleashed a tirade. Mickey, he said, was a disgrace, a drunk, a lost soul, a parasite, a good for nothing, and a louse. All the while, Mickey bowed his head and teetered. We walked back to Santa María with Don José in the lead and me behind, propping up my fellow 'pilgrim'.

By the time I reached the provincial capital of Leon, I had come nearly 300 miles and there were another 200 to go. Just ahead lay the mountains of Leon, snow-capped and wind-blown. To tell the truth, I was tired and weather-beaten. I decided to take a day off from the Way and rest my weary feet and bones. I checked into a hostel full of university students and lonely widowers.

It was wonderful to ramble rather than march for a change. I went to morning mass at the Gothic cathedral. There wasn't a very good turnout, just a handful of elderly women, a few students and me, but the young priest delivered an inspired sermon. The light of faith, he explained, was akin to the light which was just then streaming through the cathedral's sea of stained glass (12,917 square feet of it) and casting the nave in an iridescent glow. That a substance so fragile and yet so luminous as glass could withstand the weight of the stone walls was miraculous, he said. And so it was with the spirit illuminated by the Word. (In fact, the sheer quantity of stained glass in the cathedral had been a source of alarm to architects for centuries, but never mind, I got the priest's point.)

After mass, I strolled along the bank of the Bernesga river; I idled away a few hours in a café; I stocked up on some provisions; and I had a lavish lunch, followed by a long siesta. I felt renewed.

In the afternoon, I sought out the church of San Isidoro, a twelfth-century Romanesque treasure built upon the remains of a primitive Christian church which had, in turn, been built upon the remains of the ancient Roman temple of Mercury. In the narthex lay the Royal Pantheon of the medieval kingdom of Leon. When I entered the chamber I found myself transposed to a sublime Romanesque scene. Stout columns, whose capitals were carved with New Testament figures, rose up to a series of six vaults resplendent with frescos of scenes both sacred and temporal. Alongside characters from the Gospel were others from mythology. A magnificent depiction of Christ the teacher showed the Lord preaching to the Apostles. The inside of an arch was decorated with the tasks of the months. Along a rib of a vault strode a pilgrim. The distribution of subjects, the blending of figures and purely decorative motifs, and the treatment of divine and worldly themes were a masterpiece. The artist, sadly, was anonymous.

As I stood gawking, a guard approached to inform me that the pantheon was known 'in art circles' as the 'Sistine Chapel of Romanesque Art'. It was no hyperbole.

Two days out of Leon, just past the town of Astorga, the snows hit. At first it was just a flurry, but as I climbed the mountain road that led out of the *meseta* and into the bare, grey mountains of Leon, the snow began to get heavier until, by mid-morning, it had turned into a blinding storm. 'In the mountains of Leon you will freeze,' the priest at Roncesvalles had said. I cursed him for the accuracy of his prediction, and myself for having started out so late in the year. I didn't feel so much a fanatic as a fool. Then I remembered too the benediction: 'Oh God . . . be for him a companion on the march, a guide at the crossroads; give him . . . shelter along the route, shade from the sun, light in the darkness, solace in moments of discouragement . . .' By the looks of things, I would need it.

I ascended Mt Irago in a white whirlwind. I dared not stop, and even if I had, there was no place to seek shelter. If I didn't come across any refuge, there was a military base at the summit and I would have to put myself at the mercy of the Spanish armed forces.

And then I heard the distant bleating of sheep. I came around a bend to find a caped figure and a pack of dogs herding a flock out of the storm and into a barn. When the mongrels had done their task, they promptly set upon me, but one call from the shepherd and they backed off snarling.

'*Hola, qué tal?*' he asked matter-of-factly.

'Frozen,' I replied.

He invited me into his house. The snow was already shin-deep on the short path from the barn, but there was smoke rising from the chimney and I felt a rush of relief.

Inside, the wind was whistling through the cracks in the brick, the cement floor bore a patina of frost, and there was no fire-place. Evidently, the house was divided in two and the chimney belonged to his neighbour. We huddled around a butane stove.

His name was Antonio. He was from Madrid, but he had been living on the slopes of Mt Irago for nine of his thirty-four years. When he first arrived, there had been something of a commune and he had revelled in the pastoral ideal, vaguely anarchist senti-ments and free love. 'But the spirit of camaraderie', he said, 'didn't last.' Some members grew greedy and jealous, others idle. Slowly, people began to fall out. From an original group of twenty, the commune shrunk to twelve, and then to a hardened cell of seven. Gone were the anarchist good intentions and the free love; and the pastoral ideal had been reduced to the rather grim reality of tending a flock of sheep on a remote, rock-strewn slope. Finally, only Antonio and his neighbour remained, and it wasn't long before they were at odds over the division of labours. A squabble turned into a row and dislike into hatred. They divided the flock, the barn, and everything else they once shared. They built a brick wall, cutting the house in two. Antonio got the bathroom, his ex-colleague the chimney. They did not speak, not as they passed one another on their way to and from the barn, or in the pastures, or even, I gathered, in the midst of a severe storm. Although there was no one else living for miles around with whom to converse, they observed a bitter, recalcitrant silence. They reminded me less of Cain and Abel, than of Abel and Abel.

Antonio went to look in on the sheep, while I put on a pot of coffee. His dwelling was a shambles. There was a bed, a drawing table, and a bookcase fashioned from crates and planks on which I noticed much-thumbed editions of Miller's *The Tropic of Cancer*, *The Poems of Antonio Machado*, *Don Quixote* and the *Kama Sutra*. There was a photograph of a younger Antonio sitting atop a motor-cycle in Madrid's Plaza del Sol. In front of a tattered sofa lay a single layer of bricks which appeared to be the beginnings of a chimney, but the work had been long since abandoned. Alongside rose a heap of bricks and bags of mortar.

When Antonio came in from the cold, I was sitting at the drawing table, sketching some modest plans for a chimney. I had worked as a mason's assistant, I told him, and I still remembered how to tie a chalk-line, mix proper mortar, lay bricks, and strike up joints. Antonio was elated.

We worked long into the night. The best means to fight the cold was to keep moving. Fortunately, we also had a bit of whisky. Antonio sang. By the time we stopped for the night, the chimney stood waist-high. We had no level with which to check the horizontal, but nothing appeared grossly askew.

The night was painfully cold and interminable.

In the morning, it was still snowing. We waded through drifts to the barn to tend the sheep. A lamb had been born in the night, but it had quickly been crushed by the rest of the flock. Its tiny pink body lay cold in the hay. Antonio was enraged. He set about kicking the sheep around him and swearing wildly. Then he turned to me. 'My little flock, Your Father has given you his kingdom,' he jeered, quoting Luke. 'If you ask me, Christ chose the stupidest fucking animal to represent his followers.'

I remained silent. Antonio took the lamb and buried it in a drift.

At dusk, we broke through the ceiling and installed a makeshift chimney pipe of tin tubing. Antonio fashioned a flue from a baking sheet. We then proceeded to gather anything that would burn: newspaper, old crates, boxes and broken furniture, and piled it all in the hearth. Antonio passed me the matches. 'You light it, pilgrim. If it hadn't been for you there would be no chimney.' I lit some newspaper, warmed the chimney, and lit the fire. The dry wood caught fire and sputtered and crackled.

147

Smoke poured into the room, and for a moment I thought we had made a mess of it, but then the fire got roaring and the chimney began to draw like a dream. For a long time we said nothing; we just squatted in front of the flames and relished the warmth. We swigged whisky.

'Forgive me for insulting the Christians,' said Antonio suddenly.

'No need to mention it. I for one have always found the metaphor of the flock to be demeaning. But there is one thing.'

'What's that?'

'Next time,' I said only half in jest, 'don't kick the sheep.'

It stopped snowing in the night and the day dawned cloudless, but bitterly cold. All around, the landscape was white and gleaming. I gathered my things and said goodbye to Antonio. We both thanked each other profusely. I told him that he was always welcome in my home in Barcelona, but it was, I realized immediately, an invitation he could never accept: his place was with his flock.

I walked up the road towards the summit of Mount Irago. I hadn't gone 100 metres before I heard Antonio calling out 'Nicolaaaaaas!' I turned around to see him waving joyously from the barn door. 'Three new lambs!' I raised my walking stick in salute. Ribbons of smoke rose from two chimneys.

There was a small iron cross atop a wooden pole at the summit of Mount Irago. Following pilgrim tradition, and an even earlier pagan practice, I placed a stone at the base and prayed for a safe journey. The custom is said to derive from the Romans, who regarded these mountains as the domain of Mercury and from whose depths they mined gold.

All afternoon I descended the western slope. The Way ran contiguous with the mountain road which, thankfully, the military had ploughed. The sun was brilliant, but there was a vicious north wind. I wore sunglasses to avert snow blindness. The landscape was utterly desolate. I walked through the ghostly streets of abandoned villages, and for long stretches there was no sign of human life whatever. I did, however, see scores of birds of prey, circling in the azure sky, and once, the alarmingly fresh spoor of a wolf pack.

As night was falling, I crossed the Boeza river and walked into Ponferrada beneath a star-filled sky and the ramparts of the castle of the Knights Templar.

I shared the pilgrim refuge at the Basílica de Nuestra Señora de la Encina with a French pilgrim named Philippe. Outside, tethered for the night, was his mule Caline. Philippe was thirty-two, the mule twenty.

Eight months before, Philippe had quit his job in a French telephone company and set out from Toulouse with Caline, whom he had saved from the slaughterhouse. To earn enough money for his bread and Caline's oats, he played the dulcimer on church steps and in squares. He studiously wore the garb of a medieval pilgrim: a cape, a floppy hat, sandals and a staff. The beast of burden carried his supplies. He was, Philippe insisted, journeying not to Santiago, but to Compostela. His was a God of the sun, the stars, the Way, and the peaks. He never went to Mass, but he spent a good deal of time meditating and, if no one was about, smoking hashish in the churches along the route. His brother was also on the pilgrimage trail, three or four days behind, travelling with a goat.

But now Philippe was stuck. The storm had blanketed the surrounding peaks with up to a metre of snow and he feared that the wolves would attack Caline. 'I would rather turn back than see her harmed,' he said sadly. 'She is so innocent, so *fidèle*.'

I was glad not to be burdened with a beast.

*

As I climbed the final pass which leads from the ancient
kingdom of Leon to Galicia, the snows returned with a fury. By
the time I reached the hamlet of O'Cebreiro, located on the
wind-swept summit, I was numb with cold, exhausted,
thoroughly dispirited, and covered from head to foot in snow.
When I pushed through the door of the inn attached to the
pre-Romanesque church, the proprietress shrieked.

Like so many outposts along the Way, O'Cebreiro would
likely not exist were it not for the pilgrimage route. In the ninth
century, a French nobleman established a hospital for pilgrims
on the site. The hospital later became a Benedictine monastery,
and finally an inn, which it still was. Here, pilgrims had sought
succour for well over a millennium.

I ate dinner in front of the fire. But for an elderly gentleman
and his rather tarty mistress (she wore stiletto heels in the stark,
medieval dining room), there were no other guests. The
proprietress served me soup, lamb, and ink-dark wine. She was
very drunk and eager to talk.

'You wouldn't be the first pilgrim to freeze in these parts,' she
offered. 'Last year a man got caught in a blizzard and died in the
snow just outside the village. It took the military helicopters
days to find him and when they did, he was being picked clean
by birds. Around here the birds are *CARNÍVEROS!*'

After dinner, I followed her weaving frame through the
kitchen, down a corridor, and into the sacristy. She gave me an
incoherent tour of the church, including a look at the
'Miraculous Chalice', a twelfth-century relic which, she assured
me, transformed bread into flesh and wine into blood.
On the way back through the kitchen, she fetched a bottle of
whisky and poured out two hefty glasses. 'To the pilgrim,' she
managed, lifting her glass unsteadily. We drank it down in a
breath.

When I lay down to sleep, the storm was still raging, and in the next room the gentleman and his mistress were delighting in their rendezvous.

The morning was still and silent, without a wisp of wind. I took a walk around the village before breakfast. In some places the drifts were knee-deep. I shovelled the snow from the entrance of a house for an ancient, toothless widow. Scattered around the village were a number of *pallozas*, stone dwellings with sweeping, bell-shaped roofs of thatch which are prehistoric in origin. I poked my head into one and found a herd of startled Holsteins.

Back at the inn, the garrulous proprietress was terribly hung-over. She served me breakfast silently.

Just as I was setting off, however, she appeared with a picnic lunch of dried sausages, cheese, bread, and a plastic jug of wine. 'Pray for me in Santiago, pilgrim.' She then slumped back into the kitchen; the furtive couple descended the stairs smiling and ravenous; and I walked down into Galicia.

When I reached the Monastery of Samos at the bottom of the valley, the amber-coloured stone of the Baroque façade was already cast in late-afternoon shadows. I knocked at the door and heard the approach of sandals over stone. A young monk let me in. '*Bienvenido*,' he whispered. His name was Augustine. Samos was inhabited by a silent order of Benedictines, but he was in charge of the pilgrims and so was allowed the luxury of a few spare words.

He led me across a cloister lush with Old Roses, up a Baroque staircase, and down a corridor decorated with ghastly contemporary murals, to a clean and orderly cell.

At nine o'clock, I was fetched for dinner by Augustine. I entered the cavernous dining hall behind a file of eleven robed brothers; the abbot entered last. I was seated at a table alone. No one uttered a word, but one monk sat in a pulpit above the hall and manned an archaic record player. Over potato soup, grilled trout, fresh bread and wine, we listened to Bruckner's *Te Deum*. When the music reached its climax, however, the sound was distorted and deafening. The abbot reached for a bell and rang it vigorously in protest. The deejay brother couldn't seem to find the 'volume' to turn the music down; finally, he pulled the plug in desperation, and Bruckner came to a screeching halt. We finished dinner in silence.

The lights went out at ten o'clock, but I lit a candle and read Rilke until well past midnight. In *The Book of Pilgrimage* I found the precise expression for my spiritual mood:

All those who seek Thee tempt Thee,
And those who find would bind Thee
To gesture and to form.

But I would comprehend Thee
As the wide Earth unfolds Thee.
Thou growest with my maturity,
Thou Art in calm and storm.

I ask of Thee no vanity
To evidence and prove Thee.
Thou Wert in eons old.

Perform no miracles for me,
But justify Thy laws to me
Which, as the years pass by me,
All soundlessly unfold.

For three days I walked through gently rolling hills, woodlands of oak, pine and eucalyptus, and abundant mist. The apple and grape harvests had passed, but the countryside still appeared lush and overgrown. I watched farmers cutting their emerald-green fields with great sweeps of a scythe and hoisting the grass into carts borne by oxen. The men wore tweed flat caps and waist-coats; the women dressed in black and tied their hair in scarves, babushka-style. The scene reminded me less of Iberia than of Ireland, and the similarities went beyond a mere affinity for landscape.

In the sixth century BC, about the same time that the Greeks were colonizing Iberia's Mediterranean shore, the Celts arrived on the Atlantic coast in the west (the name Galicia derives from the same Celtic root as Gaul and Wales). Until they were finally subdued by the Roman invasion, the Celts thrived. I found their legacy in the primitive stone fortifications known as *castros* which dot the countryside, in the Celtic crosses which fill ancient graveyards, in the drone of Galician bagpipes and the freckled countenances common among the locals.

I passed very few towns to speak of, but rather a progression of tiny settlements which had sprung up along the Way over the centuries. Nearly all of the inhabitants in these nearly feudal hamlets were elderly. Their land had been relentlessly divided, generation after generation, until there was no recourse for the young but to emigrate in search of fortune. Now and then, I came across the dream houses which emigrants had built upon their return from years of labour in Catalonia, northern Europe, or Latin America. They were a jumble of marble and glass, polished granite and imposing wrought-iron gates, concrete balustrades and pointless fountains. That these gaudy little palaces had often been built in the shadows of humble Romanesque churches and hermitages or primitive hovels gave the impression that virtually nothing had been built in the intervening centuries. It was as if there had been an architectural hiatus of almost a thousand years.

I made a brief detour to Vilar de Donas, a Romanesque

church and former monastery which had served as a centre and burial ground for the Knights of the Military Order of Santiago. These medieval warriors had journeyed to the Holy Land on successive Crusades (nothing less than a pilgrimage under the sword), and upon their return, helped to rid the Way of the bandits and thieves who regularly preyed on the meek, hapless pilgrims.

I was amazed to find the church open. There were chickens strutting among the columns, and a cow feasting on the overgrown grass in the churchyard, but no sign of a priest or, indeed, anyone. The aisles were lined with great, carved-stone sepulchres containing the brittle bones of heroic knights of old. The apse was painted with the image of a stigmatized Christ, and although the work of the anonymous medieval artist was crude and lacked proportion, it moved me more than any masterly Baroque triptych. The church's portals were crumbling, the frescos were slowly being obliterated by time and the elements, and the tombs of the knights lay neglected, yet in the shadows of the altar stood a small table with wild flowers and votive candles strewn around a plastic Jesus.

I slept in a pew, a modest pilgrim among legendary knights and a few indifferent chickens.

When I reached the summit of the hillock called Monte del Gozo (Mount of Joy, Monjoie, Monxoi) on the outskirts of Santiago, I caught sight of the cathedral towers rising above tile roofs. The honey-coloured spires shone like beacons in the morning light. My spirits soared. More than a sensation of mild accomplishment for having marched 500 miles in 28 days, or of physical relief for a body fatigued and blistered, as I stood gazing over Santiago de Compostela from Mount Joy, I felt just that: pure, unmitigated joy.

I entered the city through the Puerta del Camino and followed a succession of labyrinthine Gothic streets to the cathedral. It was noon and the streets of Santiago were teeming. For days I had walked in virtual solitude through a wilderness both real and symbolic, and now, as I stood in the Plaza Obradoiro before the cathedral's delirious Baroque façade, I was surrounded by a throng. There was a swarm of Italian tourists just off the bus, university students rushing off to class, elderly couples feeding the pigeons, a flock of nuns taking snapshots of the lofty cathedral, and a group of shrill demonstrators protesting against Spain's obligatory military service. The square seemed to accommodate equal measures of the sacred and the profane.

I climbed the steps of the cathedral and stood beneath the Portico de la Gloria. The portal, carved with more than 200 biblical figures in the twelfth century by Master Mateo, is one of the most exquisite Romanesque works of art in existence. I made out Christ and the Apostles, the Prophets, the twenty-four Elders of the Apocalypse, and a host of angels, musicians and saints. Inside the central arch rose the heavenly Jerusalem. There were archivolts carved with scenes of the messianic promise to Adam and Eve, and the captivity of the tribes of Israel. Growing up a mullion was the Tree of Jesse. The Final Judgement unfolded with precision, the chosen to the left, the damned to the right; and in Hell, sinners were being consumed by dragons and grotesque beasts.

The portico's central column supported a figure of St James, beneath which pilgrims traditionally bow and pray before entering the cathedral. It is the last act in a pilgrim's progress. When I placed my hand on the column, my fingers found the smooth, time-worn hollows where an incalculable stream of pilgrims had placed their hands before me. I bowed my head and gave thanks.

Inside, the iconography of the Apostle was everywhere. There was St James the Moor Slayer poised with a sword held high against the usurpers; St James the pilgrim with his cape, staff, and scallop shell; and a resplendent St James cloaked in gold and studded with jewels which rose above the main altar. I waited in line with the pious and the merely curious to file through the cathedral crypt and glimpse the purported remains of the Apostle himself, stored in a silver casket and flanked by the empty tombs of his disciples St Athanasius and St Theodore. When my turn came to prostrate myself before the venerable relic, I felt strangely at a loss, as if I had come to the wrong place. It didn't much matter; a Belgian family was nudging me along, eager to catch the numinous scene on video. I scarcely had time to bless myself reflexively before I was swept along and out of the crypt.

I missed the silence and striding of the Way.

I wandered among the side chapels and found myself kneeling before the shrine of St Martin, he who divided his cloak to share with a beggar. I prayed for the widow in Burguete who had given me my walking stick, for the hotelier in Pamplona, for the bell ringer on the slopes of Monte el Perdon who had fed me, for Ramon Sostres, lonely and malnourished, for Mickey that he might find his ship, for Antonio and his neighbour that they may break their silence, and for the brothers of Samos that they may keep theirs. I thanked them all for helping me to keep a fragile, pilgrim's faith.

5 / A Sometimes Holy Land

We sat down by the streams of Babylon and wept there, remembering Sion . . . Jerusalem, if I forget thee, perish the skill of my right hand! Let my tongue stick fast to the roof of my mouth if I cease to remember thee, if I love not Jerusalem dearer than heart's content! Remember, Lord, how the sons of Edom triumphed when Jerusalem fell; O'erthrow it, they cried, o'erthrow it, till the very foundation is left bare. Babylon, pitiless queen, blessed be the man who deals out to thee the measure thou hast dealt to us; blessed be the man who will catch up thy children, and dash them against rocks! *Psalm 137*

Look, Master, what stones! *Mark 13:1*

Many a time have We seen you turn your face towards heaven. We will make you turn towards a qibla that will please you. Turn your face towards the Holy Mosque; wherever you be, turn your faces towards it. Those to whom the Scriptures were given know this to be the truth from their Lord. *Sura II*

She had fine red hair and rosy cheeks. An ill-fitting, vaguely military grey uniform hung from her almost adolescent body. She was from Security, she said, smiling. The questions which she would ask me were intended for my own safety and that of my fellow El Al passengers and crew members. It was four o'clock in the morning. Outside, the desert was unfathomably dark, but the lights inside Ben Gurion Airport were glaring. I was drawn and drowsy. Security, however, was wide awake.

'What was the purpose of your visit to Israel?'

'I have been on pilgrimage.'

'You are a Christian?'

'Yes.'

'Why are you not travelling with a group like other pilgrims?'

'When on pilgrimage, I prefer to travel alone.'

'Where have you been in Israel over the last three months?'

'In Jerusalem, Palestine, and the occupied territories.'

She winced. If I had said Judea or Samaria, there would have been no cause for alarm, but I had unintentionally blundered into a semantic morass in which Israel, the Holy Land, Palestine, Judea and occupied territories denote far more than mere geography.

'Did you speak with any Arabs?' she hissed.

'No, but with a great many Arabic-speaking Palestinians.'

'What is your occupation?'

'I am a writer.'

Again she winced. 'Will you be writing kindly of us then?' Her tone was mocking.

'Not entirely.'

She tapped my passport in her little palm and said, 'Open your bags.'

After a cursory rummage through my backpack, she went for my book bag and pulled out my notebook with a look of smug triumph. No sooner had she opened the journal than she caught sight of my name in exquisite Arabic script written on the end paper.

'What is this?' she demanded, pressing a finger hard to the inscription.

'My name. It is Nicholas in Arabic.'

'Who wrote it?'

'A friend.'

That, apparently, was enough. 'Come with me,' she barked.

I was led to a far corner of the airport where a whole swarm from Security was busy questioning, checking, and searching the belongings of other purportedly 'high risk' passengers. Apart from me, all of the other suspicious types were Palestinians or other Arabic speakers. They appeared, I thought, frighteningly silent and docile. The waifish redhead turned me over to a more senior officer. He was olive-skinned and had syrupy, almond-shaped eyes. His shirt was open to his navel to reveal a jungle of hair in which a Star of David dangled from a gold chain. When I squinted and the medallion blurred, he looked just like the Palestinians. He was a Sephardi. He was also exceedingly thorough. My bags were turned inside out. I was ushered into a cubicle and submitted to a strip search, which included, mercilessly, my rectum (Security referred to the measure euphemistically as an 'internal cavity search'). I was asked a litany of questions about my whereabouts while I was in Israel; whom I had met; and what I had heard. I answered as diplomatically as possible and feigned an utter disinterest in politics. My concerns, I told him, were strictly religious. And then he began to page through my notebook ever so slowly.

'I fail to see how my private journal could pose a threat to my security and that of my fellow passengers and crew members,' I protested. But he didn't answer me, or even look up. For a long time, he read and I squirmed. Once or twice, he shook his head and muttered something in Hebrew. A Palestinian man emerged from one of the cubicles sobbing as he tightened his belt. At last, Mr Security cleared his throat, adjusted his glasses, and began to read aloud from my journal: 'For Palestinian Christians, the Via Dolorosa is no metaphor. The cross which they bear consists of a thousand daily humiliations whose ultimate goal is to drive them from the Holy Land. Crusades were launched for less.'

I stared at the floor.

He turned to another page and continued: 'Zionism, like anti-Semitism, I find repugnant. It has condoned the seizure of land, the massacre of whole villages, and has driven thousands into exile.'

'So,' said Mr Security, 'we are driving Christians from the Holy Land; and you find Zionism repugnant.'

'And anti-Semitism,' I clarified.

'It doesn't matter. Where exactly did you get these opinions?'

'It's a long story,' I mumbled for lack of anything else to say.

'Oh, that's O K,' he replied, yawning and propping his legs on top of his desk. 'There's no rush. Start at the beginning.'

I had always imagined that my first glimpse of Jerusalem would be from the summit of the Mount of Olives. I saw myself standing in a grove on a rocky slope and looking over the Kidron Valley to a walled city containing a confusion of domes, minarets and spires. I would hear church bells, and the shrill call of the *muezzin*, and a chorus of Jewish prayers and lamentations. I would walk into the thrice-holy city through the Gate of St Stephen and climb up the Via Dolorosa, just as He had walked, to Calvary.

As it was, I entered Jerusalem in a collective *sherut* taxi. I was squeezed into the last row of seats between a kosher butcher from Rome and a young Hassid, pale and scholarly, who never lifted his gaze from his tattered edition of the Holy Writ. The middle seats were occupied by two middle-aged, hatted ladies, apparently long separated, who were carrying on a joyous conversation of reunion in rapid-fire Yiddish. In front, next to the driver, were two French nuns, crisp and pressed, from the Order of the White Sisters.

It was close to midnight and the rain was coming down in torrents. The windows of the taxi were steeped in fog and it was impossible to see anything. Outside lay Jerusalem, but mine was a blind approach, an arrival without perspective.

I got talking with the Roman butcher skilled in the rites of

Leviticus. His name was Vito. He had come to see his brother, as he did every year. Rome, he said, was a glorious city, but he always needed to set foot in Jerusalem, 'to pray, to walk the ancient streets of the Jewish Quarter, and to take care of some business'.

He had a scheme, he told me; it was still just an idea, but he had been thrashing out the details and the time had come to share it with someone, me. I felt honoured. It would be an event, he went on, that would be reported around the world, an event with repercussions for all mankind. 'I call it,' (long pause) 'the "Peace Festival",' he exclaimed. 'Imagine, there would be Palestinian dancers, Jewish folk singers, performers from Ethiopia and the Yemen, Egypt and Syria. Everyone would come together in the name of peace!' At which point the Hassid on my left interrupted his sacred reading and pronounced the only words he would utter: 'No one', he said, turning to Vito in disgust, 'would come.'

'I would,' I said.

'And all people of proper faith,' chimed one of the sisters.

'Of course,' Vito went on undeterred, 'there are still some people who don't want peace, but they are being fed lies by the politicians. Forget politics, we will achieve peace through culture and entertainment!'

The taxi let me off at New Gate. Vito gave me his address in Rome and flashed me the peace sign. 'Don't forget,' he called from the window as the taxi was pulling away, 'the Peace Festival! Tell everyone you meet!'

I walked into the dark streets of Old Jerusalem under a steady March rain. I found a room with the Franciscans of the Custody, who, since the final Crusader retreat in 1292, had tenaciously guarded the Christian Holy Places. Seven hundred years of lonely sentry duty, I thought, made them reliable hosts. Besides, I revered their founder.

★

It was still dark when I awoke to the cry of the *muezzin*: '*La
-llah illa -llah . . .*' That the call to Muslim prayer came over
crackling loudspeakers didn't diminish the purity of the message:
'God is great.' In the Muslim Quarter and throughout Arab East
Jerusalem the faithful would be kneeling and bowing towards
Mecca and offering up in prayer one of the most beautiful passages
in all the Koran:

> Praise be to God, the Lord of the worlds!
> The compassionate, the merciful!
> King on the day of reckoning!
> Thee only do we worship, and to thee do
>   we cry for help.
> Guide thou us on the straight path,
> The path of those to whom thou has been
>   gracious: with whom
> Thou art not angry, and who go not astray.

I set out through the narrow, stone alleys of the Christian
Quarter bound for Calvary and Christ's Tomb in the great
Church of the Holy Sepulchre, the most sublimely holy site in all
of Christendom.

Coming, as I was, from the Gothic splendours of Europe, and
burdened with naïve images of the Holy Places culled from a
Children's Illustrated Bible and *The Robe*, my first encounter with
the Church of the Holy Sepulchre was, well, disappointing. I
stood in a cramped courtyard in front of the twelfth-century
façade and had the impression that I was entering through the
back door. One of the two portals was bricked up and a flight of
stairs led to another entrance, also closed. I entered through the
only open portal and beneath the gaze of Israeli police slouching
against the marble pillars.

Inside, as my eyes grew accustomed to the shadows, I found

myself before the Stone of Unction, a marble slab surrounded by candelabra where the lifeless body of Christ was washed and anointed before being sealed in his tomb. An elderly woman knelt by the stone with a bag of cheap rosaries at her side and rubbed each string of beads and cross over the worn surface of the holy rock one by one. There were oil lamps burning, and candles, and bare electric bulbs suspended from what appeared to be Ottoman-era wiring, but they did little to diminish the gloom. The air smelled of incense, wet stone, and ecclesiastical antiquity. From some hidden chapel or gallery came the sound of antiphonal chanting. I heard bells and a gong, and someone shouting in Greek. A tiny Ethiopian priest, one of the descendants of the Queen of Sheba and King Solomon, shuffled past draped in yellow robes. There were brown-vested Franciscans, hooded Armenians, Copts in threadbare vestments, and a very ancient Greek Orthodox bishop with a black veil and a jewel-encrusted crucifix hanging below a tangle of white beard.

I ascended some steep marble steps to Calvary or Golgotha, that is, 'the place named after the skull'. At the top of the stairs was a Greek Orthodox chapel built over the rock of Calvary. A young priest with the severe face of a Byzantine icon led me to the altar and knelt down to show me a silver-rimmed hole where the Cross had stood. I looked into the black void and tried to conjure up the sublime sacrifice, but up marched a troop of German tourists and the sanctity of the moment was suddenly shattered. They took turns photographing each other with their hands plunged in the sacred hole, and then rushed off to the next hallowed stop on their itinerary. The priest pulled on his beard, shook his head, and lit more votive candles.

All morning I wandered about the church, searching out the sacred sites which lay hidden in a maze of dimly lit chapels and crypts, beneath crumbling domes and Byzantine arches, and in recesses and caves hewn from the rock. The gamut of shrines ranged from those whose authenticity has been confirmed by both oral tradition and modern archaeology, such as Calvary, to the historically preposterous, for example, 'Adam's Tomb'. Yet the atmosphere of the church, the air of sprawling decrepitude, the flickering light, the sound of Eastern rites and prayers, and the robed holy men jealously guarding their shrines, caused me to dwell less on archaeology than on rich religious associations. I descended to St Helena's tomb. I peered into the Prison of Christ, where the Lord and the two thieves were detained while their crosses were being prepared. I stood above the Centre of the Universe; and I visited the Copts in their ramshackle rooftop monastery. Only then did I make my way tentatively to the most holy site of all, the sepulchre itself, the Tomb of Christ, the symbol of the everlasting pledge of Redemption.

I was distressed to find the Tomb of the Lord housed in a hideous Graeco-Russian kiosk, circa 1809, which rises in the centre of the rotunda. The structure, built rather hastily by the Greek Orthodox after the devastating fire of 1808, was illuminated by votive candles and oil lamps and enveloped in a haze from the accumulated smoke spewing from silver incensories. I waited in line along with a group of spirited Mexican nuns, some grave Russian pilgrims from Gorky, and a class of Israeli schoolchildren on an excursion. When my turn arrived, I ducked my head, entered the *aedicule*, and found myself in the tiny Chapel of the Angel. The walls were close and covered with icons, embossed silver reliefs, candles, and images of innumerable angels and saints. A wizened Orthodox priest ushered me into a second, smaller chamber where I found myself stooping before a rock bench covered with a marble slab. 'This', whispered the priest, 'is the tomb of Our Lord Jesus Christ.'

I prayed briefly.

'Which religion have you?' asked the priest.

'Christian.'

'Yes, yes, but which rite?'

'Roman Catholic.'

'I will pray for you to come back to the true Church.'

'Which Church would that be?'

'Orthodox.'

'I'm afraid that I'm having a difficult enough time where I am.'

As I was filing out, I couldn't help but wonder whether all the reverence at the Sepulchre was not something of a folly. The transcendent message, after all, was 'Christ has risen!' The Tomb, for all its sanctity, was empty.

In A D 312, Constantine the Great, Emperor of Rome, received a miraculous vision of a flaming cross with the motto, 'By this conquer.' Shortly thereafter, the emperor converted to Christianity and henceforth his army marched into battle with shields and ensigns emblazoned with the image of the cross. Convinced of the power of the crucifix, the symbol of his salvation, Constantine issued orders that the True Cross and the Tomb of Christ be found. The task was entrusted to Bishop Macarius aided by Constantine's mother Helena.

Whether or not Macarius was guided by the oral tradition of local Christians or a desire to eradicate paganism is difficult to say, but after much searching, the bishop proclaimed that the site of Calvary and the Tomb was located under Hadrian's Temple of Aphrodite. By imperial order the temple was razed; a rock-cut Jewish tomb was uncovered and promptly identified as the Sepulchre of the Lord. Eusebius, Bishop of Caesarea, was a witness and describes the discovery in the *Life of Constantine*: 'At once the work was carried out, and, as layer after layer of the subsoil came into view, the venerable and most holy memorial of the Saviour's resurrection, beyond all our hopes, came into view.' Nearby, Helena, guided by a wise, aged Jew, unearthed three crosses. To distinguish which was the Cross of the Lord, a crippled woman was stretched upon each in turn. No sooner had she touched the True Cross, according to Christian lore, than she was miraculously cured.

When Constantine learned of the discovery, he immediately wrote to Macarius, ordering the construction of a magnificent church on the site of the Lord's Passion, Resurrection and Ascension. In fact, two churches were built. The round, domed Church of the Anastasis, or Holy Sepulchre, rose over the Tomb; and a second church, both larger and grander, was built over the place where the crosses were found. Between the two churches stood Golgotha.

Nothing of Constantine's churches survives. The history of the Holy Sepulchre, like that of the Holy Land, has been marked by a succession of earthquakes, fire, invasion, siege, and schism. In 614, the Persians marched into Jerusalem under Chosroes II, set fire to all the churches, and carried off the True Cross. While the Patriarch Modestus saw to the rebuilding, the Emperor Heraclius invaded Persia and returned to Jerusalem bearing the relic in triumph. Next came the Caliph Omar in 637, who claimed the city for Islam, but refrained from persecuting the Christians or from sacking the Holy Places. When he was invited to pray at the Holy Sepulchre by Modestus, Omar chivalrously declined, saying, 'If I had prayed in the church it would have been lost to you, for the Believers would have taken it, saying: Omar prayed here.' Omar's successors, alas, were less kind. In 1009, the Caliph Hakim, an Egyptian, set out to eradicate Christianity from the Holy Land; his first measure consisted of reducing the Holy Sepulchre to rubble. When word of the sacrilege reached Europe, Christendom rose up in rebellion and Pope Urban II, proclaiming 'God wills it!' launched the First Crusade. In 1099, a Christian army led by Godfrey of Bouillon recaptured Jerusalem and sang their *Te Deum* in a ruinous Holy Sepulchre.

A Latin Kingdom was established and a massive Transitional-Norman cathedral was erected, enclosing the sites of Calvary and the Tomb under one enveloping roof. And that nearly millennium-old edifice, notwithstanding the scars of fires, civil riot, pillage and ill-conceived restorations, was essentially the church which I found. At times the whole hallowed mass seemed to be teetering, borne up more by faith than solid masonry.

But even before the Crusaders had retaken Jerusalem, the church suffered a far more devastating calamity, and one that has prevented Christian unity to this day: the Great Schism. In 1054, the Patriarchs of Constantinople, Alexandria, Antioch and Jerusalem separated from their brethren in the West over the notion of Roman primacy. They adopted the title of 'Orthodox' and insisted that they represented the true faith. The dream of a Universal Church was shattered. The division led to centuries of bickering over the Holy Places, which in turn produced a status quo that defined the precise rights and every inch of holy ground that pertained to each Christian rite. Nowhere was this painful division of the Christian world more apparent than in the Church of the Holy Sepulchre, where Latin Catholics (Franciscans), Greek Orthodox, Armenians, Syrians, Copts and Ethiopians each jealously protected their terrain and, from time to time, assaulted each other over arcane, centuries-old enmities.

When I finally exited the church and emerged into the harsh midday light, the courtyard was full of pilgrims, tourists, money changers, Israeli soldiers and urchins, and a Canadian dressed in a loincloth was proclaiming to all who would listen that he was the Risen Christ. Eventually, the police escorted him away; he didn't resist, but he kept on shouting, 'Cast the blasphemers from the Temple!'

*

I spent the afternoon tracing Christ's route to Calvary along
the Via Dolorosa. The Way of Sorrows, I was surprised to learn,
ran through the *souk*, and I was offered icons, holy water, rocks
chipped from Calvary, and crosses carved from the wood of olive
trees from Gethesemane, by a slew of Palestinian Christian
merchants whose ancestors first took up the pilgrim trade around
the time of Constantine. I prayed at various of the fourteen
Stations of the Cross, but it wasn't easy; the Via Dolorosa was
packed with pilgrims, clerics, locals going about their business,
and young soldiers, who looked exceedingly nervous. I dwelt at
the Third Station, the site where, according to tradition but not
the Gospel, Jesus fell for the first time on his way to be crucified.
Those who had seen Christ perform miracles and cure the
sick were astonished at his impotence. 'Rise up!' they urged
him, 'and conquer thy enemies.' To which Jesus replied with
the words from the parable of the Good Shepherd: 'I am laying
down my life, to take it up again afterwards. Nobody can rob me
of it; I lay it down of my own accord.' In that single utterance lay
the crux of the Christian message.

In an empty lot strewn with ancient stones and rubble near
St Stephen's Gate, I watched a group of Palestinian boys 'playing'.
The smallest in the group was made to wear a *kipa*, or skullcap,
and the other boys were pelting him with stones and jeering at
him mercilessly. They couldn't have been more than eight or nine
years old, the ages of my sons, and I thanked God that neither they
nor I had been born amidst the implacable stones and immemorial
hostilities of Jerusalem. The city was touched by holiness, it was
true, but also by resentment and messianic ambition. Isaiah's
prophecy of a paradise unfolding in Jerusalem seemed hopelessly
remote:

Wolf and lamb shall feed together, lion and ox eat straw side by
side, and the serpent be content with dust for its food; all over this

mountain, my sanctuary, there shall be no hurt done, the Lord says, no life shall be forfeit. *Isaiah 65: 25*

I ducked into the Romanesque church of St Anne, said to occupy the site of the house of Anne and Joachim, Mary's parents. The church had the look of a citadel and was another example of the shifting fortunes of real estate and faith in the Holy Land. When the Muslim armies took Jerusalem in 1187 and put an end to the Crusaders' short-lived Latin Kingdom, the church was transformed into a Muslim theological school and renamed Salahiyeh, in honour of Saladin the Conqueror. For centuries the church remained a Muslim possession, until, in 1856, the Ottoman Turks presented the property, by then roof-deep in rubble, to France for services rendered during the Crimean War. The church was restored and given to the Order of White Fathers.

I sat in a pew while an invisible choir sang the 'Ave Maria' in the crypt below. The voices rang through the church, echoed off the walls, and sent my spirit soaring.

Outside the church lay the extensive ruins of ancient pools and baths. Here, the Romans had worshipped at a temple dedicated to Serapis (Asclepius), the god of medicine and healing. Their temple, however, only dated from the second century AD, when the Emperor Hadrian paganized Jerusalem and vainly gave the city the name Aelia Capitolina (from his surname Aelius). Their choice of the temple site may very well have been influenced by the earlier Christian belief that here, in the so-called Pool of Bethesda, Jesus had performed a miraculous cure.

There is a pool in Jerusalem at the Sheep Gate, called in Hebrew Bethsaida . . . there was one man there who had been disabled for thirty-eight years. Jesus saw him lying there, and knew that he had waited a long time; Hast thou a mind, he asked, to recover thy strength? Sir, said the cripple, I have no one to let me down into the pool when the water is stirred; and while I am on my way, somebody else steps down before me. Jesus said to him, Rise up, take up thy bed, and walk. And all at once the man recovered his strength, and took up his bed, and walked. *John 5: 2–9*

As I was climbing up and down the rock ledges of the pools and the ruins of a Crusader church, I came upon an archaeologist taking the dimensions of an exquisite Byzantine mosaic depicting an eight-point cross. He asked me to help him with his measurements. His face was hollow beneath a white beard. I had the sensation that he looked older than he was. We measured the mosaic's length, its width, the size of its diminutive red, black and white stones, the dimensions of the cross, and the distance of the mosaic from the surrounding ruined walls. Occasionally, the archaeologist mumbled something to himself in French. I commented on the beauty of the mosaic.

'Yes,' he sighed, 'but I am quite sure that there is something even better underneath, but what can I do? I need more investigation and I am alone.' He was searching for the Judaeo-Christian link, for evidence of an early faith in which Christianity was still solidly entrenched in the Jewish tradition. He was sure that the proof lay buried beneath the mosaic.

He wound up his tape measure and offered to take me on a tour of the ruins. We descended rock-cut steps to the ruins of the baths. The air was cool and dank and smelled of decay. We explored a water channel from the Second Temple period, a Roman cistern, and the apses of a Byzantine basilica. The Jerusalem of Christ, he reckoned, was about twenty feet below the current street level.

When we climbed out of the shadows of the ancient stones, a golden, afternoon light was touching the façade of St Anne's. We sat beneath a palm and talked about Jerusalem. He didn't like the city.

'I would have thought that for an archaeologist Jerusalem would be close to paradise.'

'Yes, but I am also a priest and in holiness Jerusalem is very far from paradise.'

His name was Herman. He was a Belgian White Father. He had only been in Jerusalem for two years; before that, he told me in a voice cracked and full of anguish, he had been in Africa for thirty years working as a missionary in Rwanda, Zaire and Burundi. He had seen the killing fields.

'Grass is green, yes, but I have seen red grass, fields full of blood and the mutilated remains of God's innocent children.'

He had lost almost everything: his flock, his possessions, and very nearly his faith. When he left Rwanda, it was with a gun to his head.

'Now, I do not want anything. I have my artifacts, my remains, my ruins.'

He hardly ever left the church compound. In two years, he had only been to the Holy Sepulchre once. 'It was like a market, a circus.' I asked him what he thought of the authenticity of the Holy Sepulchre; if, in fact, Bishop Macarius and St Helena had found the bona fide Calvary and Tomb.

'It is possible, certainly it is the most plausible site, but it doesn't make any difference to me. I believe, like Jung, that the matter of holy sites is an existential question. The Lord can be found in many places; so can Hell.'

He stared ahead blankly and was thinking, I was sure, of the fallen in Africa.

At dinner in the cavernous dining hall of the Franciscan hospice, I sat at a table full of Argentines, including a young Franciscan priest, a middle-aged couple on their honeymoon, a lady astrologer/*espiritista* from Patagonia, and Eva Perón's sister, who, like 'Evita', must have been a beauty in her youth. Now she was very frail, heavily made-up, and fawned over by an obsequious female companion-nursemaid-slave. Evidently, she was in Jerusalem to see that certain treasures which her sister had bequeathed to the Church of the Holy Sepulchre (a lamp, I believe, and a chalice) were given the prominence which they deserved, and that a plaque be unveiled acknowledging the gifts. Earlier in the day she had had a meeting with a church custodian, the outcome of which seemed ambiguous. She was shocked at the indifference and dawdling displayed by the church officials, and would have preferred, I imagined, to realize her objectives in the manner of her sister, that is, by decree.

'Why are they so slow?' she complained.

'The Church marks time in centuries,' I offered. 'Very seldom are they ever in a rush.'

'We must leave these things in God's hands,' said the Franciscan.

'Rubbish,' she said.

I excused myself and went out into Old Jerusalem for a stroll.

The streets were dark and deserted; shops were shuttered and the cafés closed. Down passages and alleyways leading to warrens of ancient dwellings, the old Christian families of Jerusalem had shut themselves in for the night. Outside the Old City, traffic filled the streets and urban life went on with its frenetic nocturnal rituals, but inside the towering walls of Old Jerusalem, reality was steeped in a different time. Here, the only concerns were antiquity, centuries-old creeds engraved in stone, and a striving for holiness. There were no theatres, concert halls, discothèques or international hotels, just a handful of modest restaurants catering to pilgrims and tourists.

I went into a pizzeria near the Jaffa Gate for a coffee. At the bar, I was approached by a young Palestinian Christian named Zak. He liked to talk to foreigners so as to practise his English, he told me. From what I could gather, his English was superb. He wanted to know, in short order, whether or not I owned a

business; if I would hire him; if I would be willing to sponsor him
for immigration; and if there was a Christian church in my neighbourhood. I answered negatively to all but the last. He looked so
crestfallen that I bought him a drink. He ordered a tequila
sunrise. When the cocktail arrived brimming with fruit,
swizzlers and an umbrella, it looked painfully out of place in Old
Jerusalem, but Zak was delighted.

For the next hour, Zak carried on a breathless monologue on
his plight. It was a desperate story. As a Palestinian Christian
living in Jerusalem, he was caught in an unenviable predicament:
to a great many Israeli Jews he was a Palestinian, uncouth at
best, at worst a terrorist. To the majority of Muslim Palestinians
he was the follower of an infidel faith. Although he had a degree
in education from Bethlehem University, it was useless, he
admitted, smiling for the first time. 'The Jews would *never*
allow their children to be taught by a Palestinian.' Most of the
Christian schools had been forced to close due to what he called
the 'Christian Flight'. Faced with a hopeless economic future,
discrimination, and the continual legal and administrative
humiliations to which non-Jews are submitted in Israel, droves
of Christian families from Jerusalem and throughout the Holy
Land, descendants of Christ's first followers, had emigrated to
Australia, Canada, the US and Europe. Naturally, they took their
daughters with them. At twenty-eight, Zak was jobless and had
no prospects of starting a family. 'All I want', he said, staring into
his tequila sunrise, 'is a life.'

In the morning, I climbed up the walls which the Ottoman
Sultan, Suleiman the Magnificent, built in the sixteenth century
and which today still enclose the Old City. Jerusalem spread out
in an architectural frenzy of golden stone crowned by spires and
minarets, cupolas and domes. The city seemed to have sprung
from the barren landscape of dust and stone like stigmata. There

was scarcely a tree to be seen, nor did I hear any birds singing. All sacred associations apart, it was not a beautiful city; its monuments were old and hallowed to be sure, but hardly beautiful, except one. On the eastern flank of the city rose the flawless golden hemisphere of the Dome of the Rock, and in its wake, all of Jerusalem's accumulated stone seemed to pale. Built between 688 and 691 by the Umayyad Caliph Abd al-Malik, the Dome of the Rock was intended to overawe the Muslim faithful with sublime beauty and to eclipse the Byzantine Christian splendour of the Holy Sepulchre. More than thirteen centuries later, it still did.

I followed the battlements past the sadly lifeless Armenian Quarter and on to Mt Sion. The neo-Romanesque church of the Dormition, built by Kaiser Wilhelm II, towered above the site of King David's tomb, and the Cenacle, where, according to Christian tradition and rather scant evidence, Jesus and the disciples shared the Last Supper. In an alley leading to the Cenacle, a man had donned the guise of King David, a tunic and robe, sandals, and a golden crown, and was plucking a harp and singing a melancholy tune in ancient Hebrew. I walked outside the wall and skirted the ruins of the City of David which clung to the Ophel ridge between the Tyropoeon and Kidron valleys. It was here that David chose to establish his capital after he had vanquished the native Jebusites:

> And now he made his dwelling in the Citadel, and called it David's Keep; he built walls round it, too, with Mello for their outer bastion. So he went on, prospering and gaining strength, and the Lord God of hosts was with him . . . No doubt could David have that the Lord had ratified his sovereignty over Israel, and made him the king of a great people. So, when he removed from Hebron to Jerusalem, he provided himself with fresh wives and concubines there, and more sons and daughters were born to him . . .
> *II Kings 5: 9–13*

I entered the walls of the Old City once again, this time
through the Gate of the Moors or the Bab el-Magharbeh, known
popularly as the Dung Gate. Just through the threshold, a small
but vociferous group of Jewish settlers was protesting for an
all-Jewish Hebron. 'Death to the Arabs, Hebron for the Jews!'
they shouted. An elderly Hassidic gentleman stood by jeering
the settlers in Yiddish and English, but his voice was drowned
out by their megaphone. I edged over to hear what he had to
say.

'These people are a plague, an embarrassment to all genuinely
Jewish people!' he fumed.

'What exactly do they want?' I asked.

'What do they want? What do they want?! They want everything, a Greater Israel, *Eretz Yisrael*. They want to drive all non-
Jews out, first the Muslim Arabs, then the Christian Arabs. They
are Zionist TER-ROR-ISTS! They have infected good Jews
everywhere with hatred. Zionism is not Judaism!' By this time he
had attracted a bit of a crowd. Passers-by stopped to hear what
this pious old Hassid had to say. The settlers saw what was unfolding and began to shriek even louder. Suddenly, a policeman
appeared and asked everyone to move along, but the Hassid didn't
want to go. He wanted to stay and quote passages from the Torah
which strictly forbid Jewish sovereignty, which command
Jews to await the Messiah and live a righteous life. But it was
impossible, the settlers' collective shrill was deafening. The
Hassid retreated, shaking a pale fist at his enemies.

It was the Sabbath and the expansive esplanade in front of the
Kottel, or Western Wall, was crowded with Jewish faithful,
tourists, and a chilling number of soldiers and police. I made my
way to a space in front of the Wall. A rabbi offered paper *kipas* to
anyone who wanted to pray, but I respectfully declined. I
listened as a rabbi nearby led his all-male congregation in prayer
(the women were praying in a separate area off to the right).
They were reciting Jeremiah's lamentations.

'Because of the Temple which is destroyed,' pronounced the rabbi.

'We sit alone and we weep!' came the refrain from the assembled.

'Because of our walls which are fallen,'

'We sit alone and we weep!'

'Because of our majesty which has passed, because of our great men who are no longer alive,'

'We sit alone and we weep!'

Others prayed privately, facing the wall and bowing their heads. They rocked to and fro and stuffed slips of paper, on which they had patiently written their prayers, into the cracks of the massive Herodian stone. Some of the young Hassidim bore the faces of saints, pale and other-worldly, with eyes blinking from behind thick glasses – the result, I imagined, of long hours spent in dim light deciphering the Holy Writ.

The *Kottel*, in fact, is nothing more than seven leagues of the retaining wall which once surrounded the Second Temple built by King Herod in the first century B C. It is all the Jews have left of the Temple which was once the exclusive site of Jewish worship. When Titus marched on Jerusalem in A D 70, the city had been mired in a vicious civil war for more than three years. Titus's conditions for a surrender were rejected and a prolonged siege ensued in which hundreds of thousands were said to have perished. When the Roman troops at last broke the Jewish defences and reached the Temple, they went, quite literally, berserk.

And since Caesar was unable to check the passionate fury of his soldiers, and the fire was spreading, he went with his generals into the Temple's holy place and saw all that was in it, which he found more wonderful than the tales of foreigners, and equal to all that we ourselves had believed and boasted; but since the flames had not yet reached the interior, but were raging in the chambers round about,

Titus rightly supposed that the shrine itself might be saved, and ran
to persuade his soldiers to put out the fire . . . but their fury was
greater than the esteem in which they held their Caesar . . . and one
of them hindered him as he ran to restrain them, and cast fire on the
gate's hinges in the dark, so that the flames leapt out from the holy
house, and Caesar and the generals retired, and no one any longer
forbade its burning; and thus was the holy house destroyed, without Caesar's assent. *Josephus,* War of the Jews.

No priest would ever again perform a sacrifice in the Temple.
The Emperor Julian, the Apostate, briefly attempted to restore
paganism, and at the same time rebuild the Temple in AD 363,
but the Jewish elders reported that balls of fire shot from the
foundation and earthquakes scared the labourers away.

And so the Temple lives on only as a lament. There is
currently a scheme to rebuild the Temple, but the organizers
must be insane. Among other things, it would mean clearing the
Temple Mount by demolishing Islam's third most sacred site,
the Haram ash-Sharif, or 'Noble Sanctuary', where the Dome of
the Rock rises above the rock altar on which Abraham prepared
to sacrifice his son Isaac. The foundation of the altar is at once
the Jewish Holy of Holies and the place from which the Prophet
Mohammed set off on his winged stallion Al-Burak on his visionary journey to Paradise. To Muslims, the place is considered the
centre of the universe, and in the contours of the ancient stone,
the devout claim to make out the footprints of the Prophet and
the handprint of the archangel Gabriel. Since Saladin con-
quered Jerusalem in 1187, the Temple Mount has been a nearly
indisputable Muslim possession, and a source of unspeakable
envy to the Jews, who watch their Abrahamic cousins bowing to
a different creed on the rock of their faith.

I walked up to the Haram ash-Sharif along the Road of the
Chains. At the entrance gate, Israeli-Arab police searched my bag

and gave me a quick body search. I walked into the sanctuary behind a pair of pilgrim brothers from Fez. They were very pious and dignified, but as soon as they glimpsed the Dome of the Rock rising up behind groves of cedars and pines, they broke into a trot, no longer able to maintain their reserve. I approached the site slowly as if on a ship coming into port. The sanctuary, a full fifth of walled Jerusalem, was as wide as a sea in which even the Dome of the Rock looked insubstantial, but as I drew progressively nearer, the dome grew in stature until it loomed above me and appeared to float on the clouds of the Jerusalem sky.

It was Islam's first great work of architecture, but its inspiration was drawn from the great Byzantine rotunda of the Church of the Holy Sepulchre, and its architects and craftsmen were not Arabs, a desert people, after all, who had been reared in tents, but Hellenized Syrians. In no Byzantine church, however, did the expression of the dome and the octagon reach such structural and aesthetic perfection. From a central circle surrounding the Rock, the structure expanded and rose in a feat of harmonious rhythm and mathematical proportion. The exterior tiles, cobalt and cerulean blue, were lustrous in the light. Along the frieze, verses from the Koran recalled Mohammed's nocturnal journey and reminded pilgrims of the sublime significance of the sanctuary which they were poised to enter.

I shed my shoes, donned delicate slippers, and shuffled from the glaring, shadowless light of the esplanade into the dim interior of the sanctuary. It was akin to stepping into Paradise. Slender white columns rose to gilded capitals which reached up to the cupola whose surface was adorned with dizzying mosaics of amphoras, stylized vegetation, crowns and stars. Faithful to Muslim law, there wasn't a single image of man or God. From the centre of the cupola a chain hung, pointing the way to the Centre of the Universe (the second such claim in Jerusalem). I

approached an intricately carved screen and gazed at the
grey rock, so dull beneath the splendid dome. Pilgrims were
circumambulating the precinct clockwise. They bent their
foreheads to the ground and gave thanks. I descended some
stairs to the cave beneath the Rock, called the Bir el-Arwah, or
'The Well of Souls', where, if one is in a fitting state of reverence,
the voices of the dead can be faintly heard and, more distant
still, the waters flowing in the rivers of Paradise. All I heard were
tourists gasping in wonder from the precinct above.

Mohammed was much influenced by the precepts of both
Judaism and Christianity, and his followers were forever aware
of Islam's spiritual debt to the rival creeds. Still, they regarded
Islam as the more evolved religion and especially sought to
convert the followers of Jesus, whom, after all, the Muslims considered the last in the line of great prophets before Mohammed
himself. In the founding inscription which ran along the surface
of the inner octagonal wall, the Muslims, convinced of the truth
and dynamism of their young faith, left an unequivocal message
for the Christians:

> O you People of the Book, overstep not bounds in your religion,
> and of God speak only the truth. The Messiah, Jesus, son of Mary, is
> only an apostle of God, and his Word which he conveyed unto
> Mary, and a Spirit proceeding from him. Believe therefore in God
> and his apostles, and say not Three. It will be better for you. God is
> only one God. Far be it from his glory that he should have a son.

As I was approaching the Al-Aqsa mosque, 'the furthermost
sanctuary', a custodian informed me that afternoon prayers were
soon to begin and that I would have to leave the *Haram*. In the
moments of intimate prayer with their creator, the Muslims did
not want to see the infidel. I walked out of the sanctuary just as
the *muezzin*'s voice came blaring from the height of the minaret

calling the faithful to prayer. I was sorry to be excluded from the rite, even if I did believe in the Trinity and the divinity of His Son.

For weeks I scoured Old Jerusalem. I climbed the Mount of Olives and spent long hours in prayer in the Garden of Gethesemane. I traced the tomb-studded Kidron Valley, where all nations will assemble before God on the day of the Last Judgement; and I paid a visit to the Garden Tomb, a tranquil place north of the Damascus Gate, where a good many Protestants, shocked at the ecclesiastical chaos of the Holy Sepulchre, choose to locate Christ's Tomb. I went to Mass in English, Russian, Armenian and Arabic, and to temple services with Sephardic Jews whose forefathers had been expelled from Spain by the Inquisition. I waded through the Koran and the Talmud; and the Bible took on a new, intimate voice as I read familiar passages *in situ*. Jerusalemites of all three faiths boasted to me of the sanctity of the holy city and just as quickly suggested the need to drive out their perceived enemy, be they Jews, Christians, or Muslims. I came to sympathize, at least in part, with a young atheist, a rare commodity in Jerusalem, who wanted nothing more than to move to Tel Aviv and leave the believers to wallow in their prophecies.

On a bright, cloudless morning, I walked out of Jaffa Gate bound for Bethlehem, six miles to the south along the ancient road to Hebron. I thought it would make for a pleasant day trip, a stroll to the Nativity. Under other circumstances it might have been, but the Israeli military authorities had decreed what is known as 'The Closure' of the occupied territories as a result of Palestinian unrest over the plans to erect a Jewish settlement atop a hillock known as Abu Ghnein (Har Homa in Hebrew) in Arab East Jerusalem. No one was going into the territories and no one was coming out. However, I had it from a very savvy Franciscan, who was adept at shepherding pilgrims throughout the Holy Land, that the soldiers at the checkpoint along the road to Bethlehem sometimes allowed pilgrims to pass. I decided to take my chances.

The road ran between barren, grey hills. Traffic was very sparse due to the closure, but scores of military vehicles passed in both directions, and buses with metal grilles over the windows full of settlers armed to the teeth. In a desolate field, a young boy was herding goats and singing.

There was traffic backed up for about half a mile as I approached the Green Line which divides Israel from the Israeli-occupied territories. The soldiers were turning away most of the cars and trucks, but the buses full of settlers and others with Christian pilgrims were being let through. I got in line with the Palestinians who were travelling on foot. They looked spooked. When I was drawing close to the checkpoint, stones began to rain down on the opposite side of the barrier. From a nearby hill, Palestinian boys were hurling everything they could get their hands on. An Israeli officer was shouting in Hebrew and two young soldiers with automatic rifles scrambled off to disperse the boys, like Goliath chasing David. Then someone from the crowd which had formed across the checkpoint of those who were being forbidden entrance into Israel, tossed a bottle at the soldiers. That was all it took. One of the soldiers began firing into the air and half a dozen of his companions took to indiscriminately swinging their rifle butts to drive back the crowd. There was utter pandemonium, but all I could do from my side of the checkpoint was gape. I could see a woman on the ground holding her bleeding head and a young man being dragged off to a jeep. The Palestinians around me began shouting and shaking their fists. I approached the soldier at the head of the line and asked him why they were beating up the crowd, to which he replied, 'Fuck

you!' in a flawless Brooklyn accent. 'But surely,' I insisted, 'these
people . . .' Suddenly he swung around and gave me a clean,
well-trained blow to my stomach with the butt of his rifle. I fell
like a stone, wheezing in the dust and unable to breath. The next
thing I knew, I was being dragged away by an elderly priest with
bloodshot eyes and albino-white hair. He helped me to my feet
and we shuffled to his van, where I sat and caught my breath
amidst a group of terrified Irish nuns. As the good sisters prayed,
the priest leaned to my ear and declared *sotto voce* with the hint
of a brogue, 'Don't ever, ever fuck with Israeli soldiers, my son.'

I began wandering back to Jerusalem, pained at not having
been permitted to visit one of the most sacred sites of my faith.
My ribs were bruised and my ego too.

A young Palestinian boy popped his head over a stone wall
along the road.

'My friend,' he said, smiling.

'Good morning.'

'I see you have trouble with Jew soldier.'

'A bit.'

'Do not worry, we have trouble every day. You want to go to
Bethlehem?'

'Yes.'

'Come. My name is Ali. I will take you.'

I climbed over the wall and followed my pint-sized guide
along a goat path which cut through an olive grove and wound
up a hill. When we reached the summit, Ali turned around and
pointed to a nearby hill. 'Abu Ghnein,' he said sadly. For as far as
I could see there were only Palestinian villages crowned by min-
arets in the landscape. We descended to the Aida refugee camp
where Ali lived. He took me to his house, a cinder-block
shambles in a dusty alley full of rail-thin dogs and half-naked
children crying. I felt as if I were being watched through
curtains, thresholds, and from the roof tops. Ali's father

appeared. His name was Abdul. He had one eye and held a baby daughter in his arms.

'Salaam Alekhum' (Peace be with you all), I said, raising my hand to my heart.

'Ahlan Wassahlan,' he said. 'Welcome.'

We went into the house and sat on a carpet. Abdul's rather bovine wife served tea and pastries thick with honey, and his nine beautiful children filed up to shake the strange visitor's hand and say '*Hallo!*' The room was immaculately clean, but scattered with broken furniture. On a wall hung a portrait of Yasser Arafat and a poster of the Swiss Alps with a pristine, story-book village in the foreground.

Abdul lost his eye in an Israeli prison. In the early days of the Intifada, Israeli soldiers burst into his house in the dead of night. They covered Abdul's head with a sack, terrorized his family, and hauled him off to an Israeli jail. For months, he said between sips of tea, his jailers tortured and interrogated him. They wanted information about the uprising in the territories, but Abdul knew nothing. He had never had anything to do with politics; he wasn't a fundamentalist; and he was certainly no terrorist. They kept him locked up for two years and tortured him periodically. During one particularly sadistic session, one of his torturers kicked him relentlessly in the head and he lost the eye. No charges were ever filed; he never had a trial.

When he got out of prison, he went to work for a construction company in Jerusalem building houses for the Jews. He had no choice, he insisted; he had a family to feed and there was no work in the territories. With the latest closure, however, he had been fired from his construction crew and now he didn't know what he would do.

I didn't know what to say.

It was getting late. Abdul told Ali to accompany me to Bethlehem. 'Pray for us when you are in the Church of the

Nativity,' he said. 'After Mohammed, Jesus is my favourite prophet.'

The square in front of the Church of the Nativity was full of tourist buses and merchants hawking rosaries and nativity figures carved from olive wood, postcards, and T-shirts printed with 'Shalom'. I overheard an Israeli guide explain to a group of American Christian pilgrims that 'As you all know, Bethlehem, or Beit-lechem as we Jews like to call it, is the birthplace of King David.' Long pause. 'Jesus was born here too.'

I entered the church and found myself before five symmetrical naves and a crush of tourists and pilgrims. I waited in line to descend to the site of the Nativity located in a cave beneath the apse. The wait was interminable. When I finally reached the hallowed spot, indicated by a silver star set in the marble floor, pilgrims were clamouring to rub the star with rosaries and prayer cards; a German stood filming the scene, and an American woman was haranguing her guide. 'I want to see the manger,' she demanded. 'The MANGER!' I said a quick prayer to Abdul and his family and fled. If Christ were among us, I thought, he would be in the refugee camp.

I walked back to Jerusalem in the twilight, taking the time to follow Ali's goat path so as to avoid the checkpoint. When I reached Jaffa Gate, church bells began to peal. I bought a palm branch from a tiny nun in the square. The next day was Palm Sunday.

At dawn, I climbed the Mount of Olives in a downpour and wound my way down the eastern slope to Bethphage, whence Christ set off for his triumphant entrance into Jerusalem riding an ass and treading the capes and olive branches with which his followers had strewn his path. I went to Mass at the Franciscan church and read from Matthew:

When they were near Jerusalem, and had reached Bethphage, which is close to mount Olivet, Jesus sent two of his disciples on an errand; Go into the village that faces you, he told them, and the first thing you will find there will be a she-ass tethered, and a foal at her side; untie them and bring them to me. And if anyone speaks to you about it, tell him, The Lord has need of them, and he will let you have them without more ado. All this was so ordained, to fulfil the word spoken by the prophet: Tell the daughter of Sion, Behold, thy king is coming to thee, humbly, riding on an ass, on a colt whose mother has borne the yoke. *21:1–5*

When I emerged from Mass, the rain had stopped and dark clouds were racing over the Mount of Olives, heading east towards Jericho and the Dead Sea. I walked back up the hill, tracing Christ's path. Church bells were echoing all over the landscape, from the Church of St Lazarus in Bethany, the Pater Noster and the Church of the Ascension on the crest of the Mount of Olives, and the far-off churches of Jerusalem. I came upon two young Palestinian boys riding a donkey to a Palm Sunday procession. They had decorated the little beast's ears and tail with palm branches and sprigs of rosemary, and spread a piece of velvet over his back. I asked them if I might ride the donkey for a short distance, just to capture the genuine pace of Christ's entrance into Jerusalem. They dismounted, delighted. The blessed beast of burden answered the tap of my heels with a bray and a laying back of ears and off we went. I bounced up and down in a trot and the boys chased alongside shrieking with laughter. Christ, I was sure, looked much more dignified.

At the summit of Olivet, I sat for a long time overlooking Jerusalem. Biblical shafts of light were breaking through the clouds and casting the city in a veil of gold. Here, for a moment at least, was the New Jerusalem, the heavenly kingdom, the *Urbs Jerusalem beata*, the *El-Kuds*, or the Holy, of the Muslims. But then the clouds cut off the light and the city's wet stone walls turned an insipid grey, walls that could never possibly hope to envelop all the sanctity which men and God have heaped upon Jerusalem.

I walked down past the tear-shaped church of Dominus Flevit and the transplanted onion domes of the Russian Orthodox Church of Mary Magdalene, built by Czar Alexander III. Behind the Church of the Agony, I met an elderly Italian Franciscan banging on a gate enclosed by high walls. He looked very agitated. I asked him if he needed any help.

'*No, grazie.*'

I asked him what was behind the wall.

'*Il Romitaggio del Gethsemani,*' he said.

It was a retreat in the garden of Gethesemane. A young woman opened the gate and I peered through the threshold to see a grove of olive trees, their wet leaves glistening like silver coins in the light.

'*Avanti, avanti,*' said the priest.

I followed him into a neat compound of terraced groves with an expansive view across the Kidron Valley to Jerusalem. The priest's name was Father Giorgio. He had started the retreat a few years back to provide a place of prayer, meditation, and '*esercizi spirituali*' in an otherwise tumultuous Jerusalem. There was a chapel, a long cinder-block structure divided into small but spotless living quarters, and a rule of silence. There was also a free room. I took it in an instant.

'Thees ees no hotel,' warned Father Giorgio, gripping my arm. '*Il Romitaggio e luogo per pregare, pregare!*' ('The retreat is a place to pray, pray!').

It was just what I needed. I had been doing a good deal of wandering, not aimlessly mind you, but wandering none the less.

Father Giorgio believed that God's grace came to those who

knew how to pray for it, and he saw to it that the day was steeped in prayer. There was morning Mass at six-thirty in the adjacent Church of the Agony, afternoons of silent contemplation before the Blessed Sacrament, Vespers at six-thirty in the evening, followed by the Rosary at eight-fifteen. Otherwise, one was free to do as one liked, silently.

The other pilgrims on retreat comprised a curious lot. There was an Italian woman named Daria who lived more or less permanently at the Romitaggio; she looked after Father Giorgio and assumed the role of Mother Hen. She helped me to follow the Italian Mass and the order of prayers at Vespers. I liked her instantly. She was an example of a lay person's capacity for godliness. Elizabeta, a French divorcee, devoted her time to travelling the world from holy site to holy site on a kind of perpetual pilgrimage. She always dressed in white and was fond of prostrating herself on the floor of the chapel and at Mass in the Church of the Agony in fits of rather self-conscious piety. Next door to my cell was a young priest from Tennessee named Father Bob. He was journeying to each and every one of the East's Orthodox Patriarchs to seek their blessing and pray with them for a unified Church. He believed, like every honest American, that with right effort *anything* was possible, even healing the millennium-old Great Schism. He was waiting for an audience with the Armenian and Greek Patriarchs of Jerusalem. Lastly, there was Antonio, a brilliant, aspiring theologian who was studying in Jerusalem. He was a *Madrileño* and we sat up long hours whispering in Spanish and discussing Old Testament prophecies, the message of the Gospels, Jerusalem, Jaspers, Jung, and our favourite bars in Madrid.

When I wasn't taken up in prayer, I stole into Jerusalem. The Old City was overtaken by Holy Week pilgrims and tourists. Compared with the silence of the Romitaggio, Jerusalem was deafening. Along the Via Dolorosa, I encountered a continual flow of tour groups being ushered along the path to Calvary like so many sheep. They called themselves pilgrims, of course, but for the most part they were engaged not in pilgrimage, but in a sort of harried religious tourism. Their routine was invariably the same. They would have come, let's say, from the US or Europe on a comfortable jumbo jet, accompanied by their familiar and reassuring parish priest. Upon their arrival at Ben Gurion airport, they would be herded into an air-conditioned bus and whisked to their air-conditioned hotel, where they would find Western amenities and, praise the Lord, Western cuisine and bottled water. An Israeli guide would lead them to the Christian sites at an infernal pace, allowing no time for things like prayer and meditation; there would be more important things on the agenda, like stopping in the bazaar and doing a bit of shopping at the establishment of the guide's choice, where, he assured the hapless 'pilgrims', they would get a fair price. And he a hefty commission. Their whirlwind, eight-day tour would take them through Jerusalem, to Bethlehem, Nazareth, and the Sea of Galilee. Then, home again. There would have been no contact with any locals, no communion with their Christian brothers and sisters who were bearing the Cross in the Holy Land. They would have had little time to pray and scarcely a moment to reflect, but they would have captured their 'pilgrimage' on video and they would watch it for years to come.

My model pilgrim has always been Egeria, a Spanish lady who crossed the breadth of the Roman Empire from Iberia to Palestine from 381 to 384. Egeria's account of the journey to the Holy Places was discovered in the seventh century by a Spanish monk named Valerius, for whom her pilgrimage was an example of saintliness:

We revere the valorous achievements of the mighty saints who were men, but we are amazed when still more courageous deeds are achieved by weak womanhood, such deeds as are indeed described in the remarkable history of the most blessed Egeria, who by her courage outdid the men of any age. Nothing could hold her back, whether it was the labour of travelling the whole world, the perils of seas and rivers, the dread crags and fearsome mountains, or the savage menaces of the heathen tribes, until with God's help and her own unconquerable bravery, she had fulfilled all her faithful desires.

I found myself staying more and more inside the silent walls of the Romitaggio, praying, meditating, reading the Gospels, and doing a bit of gardening for Father Giorgio. Seldom had I felt happier.

At dawn on Good Friday, I sat in the olive grove reading Scripture and was overwhelmed with a sense of the immediacy of the impending Passion. It was here that Christ had sweated blood as he prayed for the strength to face his preordained end, and where Judas Iscariot touched his lips to the Lord's cheek in history's most infamous kiss.

And now he went out, as his custom was, to mount Olivet, his disciples following him. When he reached the place, he said to them, Pray that you may not enter into temptation. Then he parted from them, going a stone's throw off, and knelt down to pray; Father, he said, if it pleases thee, take away this chalice from before me; only as thy will is, not as mine is. And he had sight of an angel from heaven, encouraging him. And now he was in an agony, and prayed still more earnestly; his sweat fell to the ground like thick drops of blood. When he rose from his prayer, he went back to his disciples, and found that they were sleeping, overwrought with sorrow. How can you sleep? he asked. Rise up and pray, so that you may not enter into temptation. Even as he spoke, a multitude came near; their guide was the man called Judas, one of the twelve, who came close

to Jesus, to kiss him. Jesus said to him, Judas, wouldst thou betray
the Son of Man with a kiss? *Luke 22: 39–48*

The days leading up to Easter were full of sorrow. The events
of Christ's Passion included Peter's denials, Judas's suicide by
hanging, false testimony, Pilate's washing his hands of the death
of an innocent man, the scourging and the slave's death by cruci-
fixion, and God forsaking His son. The story would be tragic
were it not for the outcome: resurrection, ascension, and eternal
life; in a word, Easter.

I went to Easter Mass at the Church of the Holy Sepulchre.
The crush of pilgrims was stifling, but there was a festive mood
and a Babel of tongues. Mass was celebrated in front of Christ's
Tomb in the Rotunda. A dais had been set up to accommodate
the Latin Patriarch and a host of cardinals, bishops, monsignors,
and assorted dignitaries. There was a great deal of pomp, clouds
of incense, and the rustle of rich vestments. All the trappings and
arcane rites were mesmerizing, but I was also gratified to find a
Church clamouring for social justice. Michel Sabbah, the first
Palestinian Christian to be named Latin Patriarch of Jerusalem,
gave the homily. The local Christians in the crowd hung on his
every word:

'Saying peace, peace, whereas there is no peace' [he said, quoting
the Prophet Jeremiah]. The paths of peace are not the paths followed in these days. God gives the authority to the governors to
obey the laws of God and to impose laws which produce justice,
peace, and faith in God. God has promised this land for the salvation of all peoples of the earth. God has commanded justice, compassion, and equality of all. God does not command any people to
sacrifice oneself for another people. The law of force is different
from God's law. God's law means liberation of all peoples. The

liberation of the Jewish people, in the Bible, was the image and prefiguration of the liberation of all peoples, including the Palestinian one. In the first Pesach, of the Exodus, God has given back freedom to the Jewish people. Today, the Jewish people cannot celebrate their freedom and their Pesach, while they keep in servitude another people, the Palestinian people.

For that, brothers and sisters, we pray: for the salvation of all the country, of all its inhabitants, Israelis and Palestinians, Christians, Moslems, and Jews. Salvation and Resurrection mean that we should form, one day, one family of the Holy Land, each one having the same rights and the same duties, no one inferior, no one superior. History has passed here and will not go back. It has left in this country two peoples and three religions: they will remain in it. No one can make the other disappear. The vocation of each one is to live with the other and for the other . . . Amen.

When Mass was over, the congregation burst into a chorus of 'Christ has risen!' The church bells pealed and we sang 'Dominica Paschae in Resurrectione Domini' alongside the empty tomb, symbol of hope everlasting.

I left Jerusalem and headed north through the Jordan river valley to Galilee. The valley was a patchwork of irrigated fields and windbreak groves of date palms and acacias. There were also clusters of jujube (*Ziziphus spinachristi*), a spiny tree of yellow flowers and succulent red fruit whose thorns were used to fashion Christ's crown of mortification. I passed beneath Mount Tabor, through Nazareth, and on to Cana, the sites of the Transfiguration, the Annunciation, and Jesus's first miracle (and my favourite), the changing of water into wine. At the Horns of Hittin, I tried to envision the blunder in 1187 of twenty thousand Christian troops marching over the parched plain under an infernal July sun and being slaughtered by Saladin's forces, in a battle that marked the beginning of the end of the Crusaders' Latin Kingdom of Jerusalem.

By the time I reached the Sea of Galilee on a crystalline morning in early May, I was eager to delve into the message and scene of Christ's early ministry. Behind me lay Jerusalem, unforgiving and sun-baked, the site of betrayal, murder, schism, and limitless ambition. Now I was entering the landscape of gentle, verdant hills enclosing the biblical sea, where Jesus sought his first disciples among a band of simple fishermen, telling them, 'Come and follow me; I will make you into fishers of men.'

At the Franciscan monastery at Tabgha, I found a dissolute friar who looked after the grounds and tiny Church of St Peter. He let me sweep out a corner of a shed as my living quarters. I stayed on for two weeks, exploring the scenes of miracles and parables which unfolded on and around the lake. Here, Christ multiplied the loaves and fishes, and walked on the water, and resurrected the daughter of Jairus, and cast the demons from a man possessed and let them consume a herd of swine, 'whereupon the herd rushed down the cliff into the lake, and were drowned'.

But it was on the slope of the Mount of the Beatitudes that I spent most of my time praying and reading the Gospel. Herman, the White Brother archaeologist from the Pool of Bethesda, had told me of a diminutive cave which cut into the slope, where, he was sure, the Lord and his disciples must have sought shelter; and it was there that I passed long hours in silent contemplation, gazing out over the lake and watching the surface of the water turn from dull lead to polished silver with the shifting light. Over and over again I turned to what is perhaps my favourite scriptural passage, uttered two thousand years before while Christ and his disciples took in the same landscape. This is what he told them:

Blessed are the poor in spirit; the kingdom of heaven is theirs. Blessed are the patient; they shall inherit the land. Blessed are those who mourn; they shall be comforted. Blessed are those who hunger and thirst for holiness; they shall have their fill. Blessed are the merciful; they shall obtain mercy. Blessed are the clean of heart; they shall see God. Blessed are the peacemakers; they shall be called the sons of God. Blessed are those who suffer persecution in the cause of right; the kingdom of heaven is theirs. Blessed are you, when men revile you, and persecute you, and speak all manner of evil against you falsely, because of me. *Matthew 5: 3–11*

More than once I tried to imagine what would have arisen had Christ remained in Galilee, preaching to a faithful following until a ripe old age, and the dark events of Jerusalem had never transpired. But it was, I realized, a joyless reflection. Without the rebellion in the Temple, Judas's fateful kiss, Pilate's acquiescence before the mob, the terror of Golgotha, and the empty tomb, the life of Christ would have been that of a wise man, even a man of miraculous powers, but not the Son of Man, the Word made flesh, or the Saviour.

6 / To Rumi's Tomb

Come, come, come again,
whoever you may be,
come again, even though
you may be a pagan or a fire worshipper.
Our Centre is not one of despair.
Come again, even if you may have
violated your vows a hundred times,
come again.

The summons, I found, was irresistible, falling as it did on a spirit
and a mind made weary by the insistent claims of the orthodox,
impervious defenders of the 'true' faith, and a catalogue of prophecies which I had encountered on a host of pilgrimages. I had
none of the fire worshipper, perhaps a bit of the pagan, and
everything of the mortal who has violated his vows a hundred
times, and more. And so I journeyed to ancient Anatolia, where
those tolerant words were dictated in exemplary and erudite
Persian nearly eight centuries ago. The author was born
Jelaluddin Balkhi; he would later earn the title of *Mevlana*, 'Our
Master', but most readers simply know him as Rumi, the
founder of the Sufi order of whirling dervishes known as the
Mevlani. It was to his tomb in Konya, Turkey, that I went to pay
homage, not as I would have to that of a prophet or a saviour,
but with all the reverence due to the Sufi whose mystical poetry
and message of love are a paradigm of the spiritual heights of
which man is capable.

In fact, Rumi didn't want a venerated tomb. 'Look not for my grave in the earth, but in the hearts of my devoted seers,' he said before his death. His followers, evidently, thought otherwise. When Rumi died on 17 December 1273, his funeral procession along the streets of Konya attracted a multitude. In a gesture telling of the mystic's ecumenical appeal, his coffin was alternately borne by his Muslim dervish disciples, Christians, Zoroastrians, and pantheists. He was buried alongside his father, Bahauddin Walad, also a theologian and mystic, in the gardens of the Seljuk Sultanate. The Sultan Velad was his son.

A mausoleum was built above the tombs of Rumi and his father and it was here that the members of the Mevlani Order came to pray, dance, play music, and pore over the Mevlana's words. Soon, annexes were added, a mosque, and a monastic centre, or *tekke*, for the dervishes. In time, the Mevlani complex became one of the most dynamic spiritual centres of the Otto-man Empire and a font of Sufism. The brightest young men *and* women knocked at the door of the *tekke*, seeking admission to the dervish order; Sultans and travellers, emirs and philosophers, the poor and the enlightened bowed before Rumi's tomb; and the Mevlani dervishes danced their whirling dance of prayer.

I stood in the courtyard of the Mevlana Mausoleum, blinded by the light reflecting off white marble and limestone. There were roses blooming in neat parterres, fountains filling reflecting pools, and Muslim pilgrims snapping pictures of domes, min-arets and Ottoman portals. Above the threshold which led to the mausoleum, a Persian inscription in gold relief was carved into the lintel:

> This station is the Mecca of all dervishes.
> What is lacking in them is here completed.
> Whoever came here unfulfilled,
> Was here made whole.

A Mecca for the mystics. I was glad to hear it, especially since as a non-Muslim I had been barred from making the *hajj* pilgrimage to the Ka'ba shrine at Mecca, arguably the world's most emblematic pilgrimage. Still, there was something sad about the inscription as well. There were no dervishes about; the *tekke* had been turned into a museum; and when the *sema* dance of the dervishes was performed once a year on the anniversary of Rumi's death, the dancers were no longer dervishes whirling in ecstatic prayer, but government employees engaging in a well-scripted pantomime under the guise of folklore. The seven-hundred-year history of monastic discipline and mystical rites of the Mevlani Order came to an abrupt end in 1925, when Kemal Ataturk, father of the modern Turkish Republic which emerged from the crumbling foundations of the Ottoman Empire, decreed the mystic orders banned and their *tekkes* closed. Since then, the Mevlani Centre has been a museum and a monument, but a thoroughly lifeless one, and I found no more tragic or telling an image than that of a wax dummy Mevlani dervish clad in his brown cloak and high, tube-shaped hat set up as a display in one of the former monastic cells.

When the cry of the *muezzin* called the faithful to their midday prayers from the nearby Selimiye Mosque, Muslim pilgrims and tourists poured out of the mausoleum. I left my shoes with a stooped guard and made my way to Rumi's tomb in stockinged feet and alone. I passed through a small domed chamber which had once been used as a Koranic reading room. The walls were crowded with inscriptions and calligraphic panels of rare beauty. In a display case were a series of heart-shaped leaves decorated with passages from the Koran rendered in gold. I continued on through silver doors and entered the central hall of the mausoleum. The room stretched beneath three massive domes, and velvet and silk-draped sarcophagi lay in rows on raised daises to the left and right. Here were the tombs of Rumi's most devoted followers and descendants and, according to tradition, those of the Horasanian dervishes who accompanied Rumi, his father and family on their flight from Balkh in Persia and the Mongol hordes under Genghis Khan. A panel bore an inscription by Rumi: 'Appear as you are or be as you appear.'

When I reached the corner in which Rumi's tomb lay, I found a young woman crying, but when she saw me approach, she covered her face with her scarf and fled, sobbing as she went. Behind a low gate of silver latticework rose the marble sarcophagus of Rumi and that of his son the Sultan Velad, draped in a black silk shroud embroidered with Koranic verses. The tomb of Rumi's father stood at the foot of those of his son and grandson. Atop the sarcophagi were stone renditions of the Mevlani's tubular headdress (symbolizing the tombstone of the ego) wrapped in the turban of the Order. Above soared a pyramidal dome. The walls were decorated in a dizzying composition of tiles and carved reliefs with floral motifs, passages from the Koran, and the words of Rumi. Everywhere there were candelabra in gold and silver, precious oil lamps, and crystal chandeliers, all donated by admirers of the Mevlana who wished to give back to Rumi some of the light with which he had instilled them.

I wandered through the rooms which had once served as the Mevlani's dance hall and mosque and gazed at illuminated manuscripts and Mameluk vases, ivory and mother of pearl lecterns and priceless carpets. One display case was devoted to the Mevlana's clothes and contained, in addition to his turban and nightcap, some silk and cotton gowns and cloaks of an elegance that would make any contemporary fashion designer flush with envy. In a gallery exhibiting countless Korans, each more beautiful than the last, I watched two gentlemen praying around a display case. When they moved on, I stepped over to see what it was they were venerating. Beneath the glass was a

mother of pearl reliquary chest; the plaque read:
MOHAMMED'S BEARD.

When I emerged from the mausoleum, the courtyard was
bathed in a warm, autumnal light and a young couple were
drinking from the fountain whose water is said to bestow blessings on the newlywed. They were very proper and formal with
one another, no groping or silly chatter, but they were clearly
very much in love. I could see it in their eyes. The Mevlana was
right, I thought: his legacy didn't lie in a tomb, but in the hearts
of God's children.

For days I divided my time between a shoddy hotel and the
mausoleum courtyard, where I spent hours sitting on a stone
bench and revelling in the mystical writings of Rumi. His output
was immense. The six-volume *Mathnawi*, Rumi's most celebrated work, consists of 5,618 couplets and took a full forty-three
years to complete. There are volumes of odes and quatrains,
letters and sermons, and a collection of discourses with the enig-
matic title of *In It What Is In It*. I stuck mostly to the *Mathnawi*
and *The Diwan of Shams of Tabriz*, a work which Rumi dedicated
to the mysterious dervish who changed the Mevlana's life,
inspired him to write his greatest mystical poetry, and was sub-
sequently murdered by some of Rumi's disciples in an act of fatal
jealousy. The scope of Rumi's field, I discovered, was virtually
limitless. He could treat the mundane and the esoteric with
equal subtlety, and imbued all of his writing with a wisdom
illuminated by the Sufi's notion of love and the continuous
quest for union with the divine. Here, Rumi on 'Quietness':

> Inside this new love, die.
> Your way begins on the other side.
> Become the sky.
> Take an axe to the prison wall.

Escape.
Walk out like someone suddenly born into colour.
Do it now.
You're covered with thick cloud.
Slide out the side. Die,
and be quiet. Quietness is the surest sign
that you've died.
Your old life was a frantic running
from silence.
The speechless full moon
comes out now.

Although Rumi was firmly rooted in the Islamic faith (his
family descended from Abu Bakr, Mohammed's companion), he,
like other Sufi mystics, was always striving towards a
communion with God which clearly superseded the doctrines
and dogmas of organized religion. To me, Rumi's message of
tolerance and his ecumenical spirit in matters of faith seemed
prophetic and, at the same time, thoroughly contemporary.
Creeds, theology, debate and exegesis interested him little; it was
the inner journey that counted:

Only Breath

Not Christian or Jew or Muslim, not Hindu,
Buddhist, sufi, or zen. Not any religion

or cultural system. I am not from the East
or the West, not out of the ocean or up

from the ground, not natural or ethereal, not
composed of elements at all. I do not exist,

am not an entity in this world or the next,
did not descend from Adam and Eve or any

origin story. My place is placeless, a trace
of the traceless. Neither body or soul.

I belong to the beloved, have seen the two
worlds as one and that one call to and know,

first, last, outer, inner, only that
breath breathing human beings.

Or this:

Cross and Christians, end to end, I examined. He was not on the
Cross. I went to the Hindu temple, to the ancient pagoda. In neither
was there any sign. To the heights of Herat I went, and Kandahar. I
looked. He was not on height or lowland. Resolutely, I went to the
top of the Mountain of Kaf. There only was the place of the ʿAnqa
bird. I went to the Kaaba. He was not there. I asked of his state from
Ibn Sina: he was beyond the limits of the philosopher Avicenna . . . I
looked into my own heart. In that his place I saw him. He was in no
other place . . .

I was beginning to wonder if all my incessant wandering of
the pilgrimage trails had been in vain.

As I was sipping tea one morning in a rather bleak café, I was
approached by a young stranger.
'You have been spending a great deal of time at the Mevlana's
tomb,' he announced without introduction.
I nodded.
'And what have you found there?'
'A very lovely museum.'
'But you are not here to visit museums.'
'Not exactly.'

He handed me a piece of paper with an address on. 'You will come this evening after prayers,' he stated roundly. 'Do *not* be late. Come alone.'

And with that he turned and walked out before I could so much as ask to what I had been so graciously invited and by whom.

I lurked in front of the house at the appointed hour. It was very dark and cold. I felt, I must admit, a tinge of fear. I thought of turning back. And then a man appeared from the shadows.

'Why do you not enter when you know we await you?'

'I wasn't sure I had the right house,' I said by way of an excuse.

He motioned to me to follow him and we walked into a dimly lit courtyard. In front of a door of a small building there were dozens of shoes in neat rows. We took off ours silently and went in. We entered a room where perhaps fifty men, young and old, were engaged in prayer, bowing towards Mecca. I took a place in the last row at the back of the room. I wasn't quite sure what to do. I thought I would be a mere observer, but an old man at my side pulled me down to my knees. I found myself bowing my head to the ground and mumbling something vaguely Arabic sounding, following along as best I could. The room was very hot and close and smelled of men. I recognized one of the guards from the museum and a pharmacist who had sold me aspirin. Some of the men were well dressed and distinguished looking, others appeared more humble. When the prayers were over, I was approached by the young man who had invited me.

'Welcome, brother,' he said, embracing me.

'Good of you to ask me,' I said, still not sure exactly where I was.

'Come, I will introduce you to the sheikh.'

I knelt before a wizened man with sparkling eyes. He offered me his hand to kiss. I obliged. He spoke in Turkish to my mysterious escort.

'He wants to know why you have come to Konya?'

'To find Rumi,' I answered. My response was translated for the sheikh and he nodded and said something else, smiling.

'He says that you have come to the right place.'

Again, I thought of the Mevlana's words: 'Look not for my grave in the earth, but in the hearts of my devoted seers.'

We sat in a wide circle. A place was made for me beside the sheikh. Tea was served and *lochum* sweets. Everyone seemed to be watching me. I smiled unconvincingly. Into the room walked a young dervish dressed in his black cloak, white shirt (his ego's shroud), and his high, felt headdress (his ego's tombstone); behind him filed in musicians bearing flutes, drums, and a sort of large tambourine. I was, I suddenly realized, about to witness a clandestine Sema ceremony.

We began with a prayer, the 'Nat-i-sherif' in praise of the Prophet Mohammed. Then a drum sounded, followed by a high-pitched whining from a reed flute which, my escort whispered, represented 'the Divine Breath'. The dervish dancer then rose, bowed to the assembled and prostrated himself before the sheikh and kissed his hand repeatedly. The music began to pick up pace and a chant rose up from the circle, 'Allah hu Akbar' (God is Great). Ever so slowly the dervish began to whirl. He lowered his arms from his shoulders to his waist and raised them again out-stretched. His right palm was turned heavenward to receive God's beneficence, his left palm to the ground, giving his Divine gift to Man. His skirts seemed to take flight and undulated like a wave as he whirled. His eyes went blank, his head tilted, and he seemed lost in ecstatic union. A small boy stood up from the circle, followed the same sequence of salutations, and began to whirl as well. He couldn't have been more than eight or nine years old. The chanting grew louder and more feverish, and the circle swayed and jerked in unison. Others joined the dancing. The chant then shifted to 'Al-lah, Al-lah, Al-lah . . .' Men beat their hearts and wailed. The music crescendoed to a climax. I grew delirious. And then the dancers suddenly whirled to a stop, the music ceased and everyone murmured 'Hu', which is all the names of God in one. There was a brief intermission and then the prayers, music, dancing and chanting started up again. Four times we chanted and the dancers whirled and each time the ceremony grew more frenzied until eyes rolled and sweat poured down ecstatic faces, and the chanting became hoarse. If Rumi chose the Sema as a vehicle designed to bring the Seeker into contact with the mystical current, I thought, by the look of it, it worked.

We ended with a reading from the Koran: 'Unto God belong the East and the West, and wherever you turn, there is God's countenance. He is All-Embracing, All-Knowing.' Then we prayed for the peace of the souls of all Prophets and all believers.

There was more tea and sweets and some informal discussion, the centre of which, it appeared, was me.

'Why,' asked one of the men seated near me who had bellowed above all the rest in his wild chanting, 'did you refuse to chant "Allah"? Are you an unbeliever?'

'I am a believer, but I was unfamiliar with the rite. I remained silent out of respect.'

'We revere Jesus as a Prophet,' said another. 'Why can't you Christians accept Mohammed as a Prophet?'

'My sacred book, as you know, ends with Christ's resurrection. Mohammed came later, he does not figure in the Bible.'

'But God sent Mohammed with a new message because Christians had corrupted Jesus's words. Islam is the more perfect faith. Surely you must see that.'

'Very few sacred words have not been corrupted by Man. The

extent to which Christianity has corrupted the words of Jesus is open to debate. Still, I believe in the Christian message which, in the final analysis, is a message of love, not unlike that of the Mevlana.'

'But the Mevlana was a Muslim!' someone shouted.

I was beginning to feel just a bit intimidated. It was more or less fifty faithful against one infidel. I looked to the Mevlana for defence.

'When will you cease to worship and to love the pitcher? When will you begin to look for the water?' I said, quoting Rumi. There was no reply, but the sheikh was smiling and nodding his head. 'We all seek God's salvation,' I continued. 'If on the Judgement Day a good and pious Muslim and an equally good and pious Christian stand before God, would it be in the nature of the Almighty to reject the Christian?'

More nodding of heads.

The sheikh pronounced the gathering over. We stood up and the modern-day Mevlani formed a line to bid the Christian good night. I kissed fifty men on both cheeks and the sheikh on his hand.

'You must come to see us again, young Christian,' he said. 'We will study the Koran.'

'And the Bible,' I insisted, 'and St John of the Cross, and Gerard Manley Hopkins, and Emerson.'

I walked back to my hotel in the dark, past the street sweepers and the last merchants closing up shop. When I got to my room, I drew the shades and began to whirl, but after a few brief turns I became hopelessly dizzy, lost my balance, and hit my head on a lamp. I settled into bed and turned to Rumi:

One went to the door of the Beloved and knocked.
A voice asked, 'Who is there?'
He answered, 'It is I.'

204

The voice said, 'There is no room for Me and Thee.'
The door was shut.
After a year of solitude and deprivation he returned and knocked.
A voice from within asked, 'Who is there?'
The man said, 'It is Thee.'
The door was opened for him.

I had been knocking, I realized, until my knuckles were raw and swollen. It was Rumi who showed me that I had been knocking from inside and that all along the door had been open.